AFALCONGUIDE®

Mountain Biking
Texas

Christopher Hess

FALCON®

GUILFORD, CONNECTICUT
HELENA, MONTANA

AN IMPRINT OF THE GLOBE PEQUOT PRESS

_A_FALCONGUIDE®

Falcon and FalconGuide are registered trademarks of The Globe Pequot Press.

Photos by Christopher Hess

ISBN 1-7627-1155-8

Manufactured in the United States of America
First Edition/First Printing

To my wife, Cathy, for her patience and her prodding during the researching and writing of this book. And to brothers Eric and John for their companionship and inspiration on the bike.

Contents

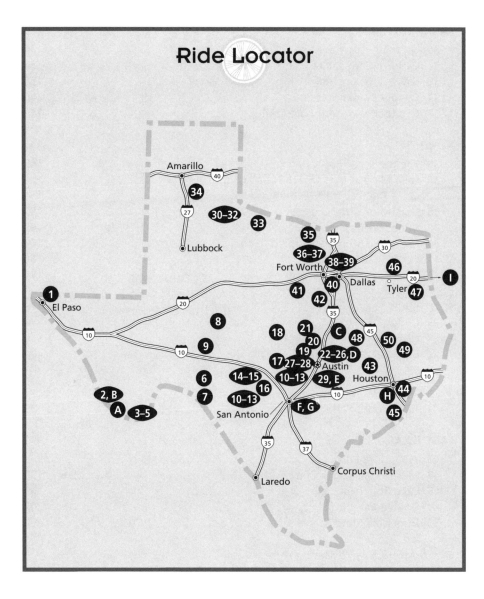

Ride Locator

Amarillo
34
30-32
33
Lubbock
35
36-37
Fort Worth 38-39
46
40 Dallas
Tyler 47
41
42
I
El Paso
8
18 21
C
45
48 50
9
20
49
19
17 27-28 22-26,D
Austin
43
6
14-15
10-13 29, E
Houston
2, B
7
10-13 16
44
A
3-5
10-13
H
San Antonio
F, G
45
Laredo
Corpus Christi

Acknowledgments

First and foremost, I would like to acknowledge all the fine folks at the Texas Parks and Wildlife Department. In flipping through the pages of this book you'll no doubt notice that the majority of the rides are on state park land. In a state that's well over 90 percent privately owned, public land is to be treasured and guarded, and the people charged with the care of our parks system do a good job of it. The recent surge in the popularity of mountain biking has brought flocks of freaks in spandex and helmets to parks around the state, and the employees and volunteers at Texas's state parks have been, almost without exception, exceedingly courteous and helpful.

On that same note, this book would not be as big as it is without the aid of a number of friendly neighborhood bike shop employees who volunteered time and coveted trail information, sometimes risking the exposure of their own beloved trails to the general mountain biking public. Bicycle Sport Shop in Austin, Crazy Cat Bicycles in El Paso, Southwest Golf and Sport in Cleburne, Desert Sports in Terlingua, and Bike World in San Antonio were particularly helpful. Thanks, guys and gals.

To all you noble souls who contribute your own time and sweat and toil to the building and maintenance of the biking trails in your community, I and every other mountain biker in this nation owe you hearty and sincere thanks. It is due to your efforts that we do what we do—namely, ride. So thank you very, very much. We should all be more like you.

Thanks to Peggy O'Neill-McCloud for giving me the opportunity to embark on a project as horrifying and fun as the writing of this book. Thanks to Erin Turner and Paulette Baker for all their help and understanding in seeing it through. And thanks to my boss, Lisa Fleck, for allowing me the freedom of scheduling necessary to roam this gigantic state from one end to the other, over and over again.

Thanks to Chuck Cypert, whom I've never met but whose book provided much guidance in getting me going.

Thanks to riding buddies Dan and Tony and Sara and Greg in Austin, Tom and Jerome in Houston, Bob and Chris in San Antonio, and Keith in Dallas, not to mention all those courteous and anonymous riders who helped me along on so many unfamiliar trails. Thanks to my mom and dad for their support. Thanks to hometown hero Lance Armstrong for the inspiration. And, of course, thanks to you, for riding.

Map Legend

Interstate		Interstate	(5)	(55)	(555)
U.S. Highways		U.S. Highways	[5]	[55]	[555]
Miscellaneous Roads (Paved)		State Roads	(5)	(55)	(555)
Gravel Road		Forest Roads	[41]	[416]	[4165]

		Cities	Capitol	Large	Small
Unimproved Roads			✹	◉	○
Selected Route		Trailhead			🅣
Optional Route		Parking			🅟
Pipelines		Picnic			
Powerlines		Ranger Station			
Fence		Rest Room			
State Boundary		Overlook			
River/Creek		Mountain / Peak			▲
Lakes/Large Rivers		Structures			■
Cliffs		Campground			
Tunnel		Gate			•—•
Boardwalk		Cemetery			†
Spring		Bridge			
Directional Scale	N				

0 — Miles — 1

Get Ready to Crank!

Contrary to popular belief, there are mountains in Texas. And hills, and canyons, and all other manner of places that beg for a bike to ride them. It isn't all desert and tumbleweeds here, and anyone who's ever planted himself or herself on a bicycle seat and set out to explore one of the thousands of tiny corners of open space in the Lone Star State knows it. Texas has everything: endless plains and rolling hills, mountain ranges and deep canyons, piney forests and boggy swamps. It's also got trails—miles and miles of trails weaving their way across the vast and varied terrain through some of the toughest, prettiest, and wildest spots in the nation. And, yes, we do have desert and tumbleweeds, and it's fun riding in those places, too.

Mountain biking in Texas can be frustrating, though. Take a drive down any desert highway or along any road winding through the Hill Country and you will be utterly agog at the endless possibilities for off-road biking. It's an endless spread of wide-open land out there, and, considering the ubiquity of cattle in the state, narrow strips of bare brown earth are often already running up the side of most hills or down into most ravines, calling, beckoning. Cattle trail? Deer path? Hell no, son, that's singletrack! But there's a problem. Back when Anglos were spreading across this great land in a swarm from east to west, Texas was carved up, sold off, and fenced in. The multiple strings of barbed wire serving as borders between these parcels of land are taken very, very seriously.

WHAT TO EXPECT

Contending with the horrible dearth of public land is the biggest obstacle for any mountain biker in Texas. The land seems infinite, but you can't touch most of it. However, a movement in recent years, brought on largely by hard times in the cattle ranching industry, has seen many ranchers realizing the value of the land to species other than cattle—namely, us. They've cut trails, planted signs, opened the gates, and charged admission, and the results are fantastic. Rocky Hill, Bluff Creek, X-Bar, Flat Rock—these are a few of the growing number of places we can now explore, and the trails are all great.

And for those vast tracts of land on which we are not welcome, there is only one thing to do: *Keep out!* It's for your own good, and for the good of our sport. The chances of more land opening to us diminish if one rancher tells another about the litter we left behind at the campsites, or the cattle we spooked and chased across the pasture, or the hikers we sent flying into the bushes because they didn't hear us coming, or the equestrian who was thrown from a horse shying from our rapid and unannounced arrival.

Not bad for a "road ride," huh? The jeep roads at Big Bend Ranch State Park make for some grand fat-tire adventure.

Etiquette is very important. Yield the trail to hikers and to horses. The future of the sport depends on it.

Now, regarding safety. I am very fortunate in that my first and most profound lesson in bicycling safety came to me by way of someone else's experience. I'd just relocated to Austin from the tame prairies of Illinois and couldn't wait to get out there and test my metal—in the form of a hulking Diamond Back beast that must have weighed every bit of thirty-five pounds—on the sweet singletrack in the heart of my newfound home.

I was living on my older brother's couch (for which I don't think his now ex-girlfriend has ever forgiven me), and one Saturday we rode down to Zilker Park to spend a day on the trails. This was when we wore cutoffs and Chuck Taylors and baseball caps turned backward against the wind when we rode trail. Approaching the trailhead we saw a couple guys leaning against their car in the parking area, one of them holding a wadded up red towel against his head. As we rolled past, we saw that the towel was filled with ice and was a once-white towel that had turned bright red with the blood that flowed from his head wound. That image has never left me.

That's right, they weren't wearing helmets. And neither were we. Needless to say that was not the fastest I've ever gone on what has become my home trail. And that was the last time I rode off-road without a helmet on my head.

A trail that some consider so tame in reality has an infinite number of potential pitfalls that can turn a fun day on the bike into a lifelong condition. This applies to every trail, everywhere. Wear a helmet when you ride your bike; it's that simple. You'll be doing yourself and everyone who calls you friend a big favor.

Protective eyewear and gloves can also go a long way toward keeping you fit and healthy. Branches always seem to be eye-high and pointing in your direction, and any time you are forced to leave the bike via the air, your hands go out to break the fall. Protect yourself, and live to ride another day.

Keep in mind that your own safety is not the only thing to consider. Public land in Texas is heavily used, and chances are good that while you're out bombing down some trail, there are other people out there who are moving in a different direction, at a slower pace, or on a different mode of transportation; your recklessness can cause them great harm. We have an advantage on a bike. They're easy to control—and they're fast. Yield the trail to pedestrians and to horses at all times. Yield the trail to oncoming cyclists when you can, and hope that they are courteous enough to do the same for you when you can't. There are few enough trails to ride in this state without risking losing access to some of them due to self-proclaimed gonzos or hammerheads. These people are idiots and should not be imitated. Life is not a North Shore free-ride video, and most public trails should not be approached as such. Use good judgment and common sense, be polite, and there shouldn't be any problems.

When riding in Texas, you should always be aware of the weather. Keep an eye on the sky for building storms, as many open areas where we ride are prone to flash flooding. These things happen so fast that you will not have time to react. Better to preempt the problem by being aware and staying out of harm's way. If it's been raining and the trails are muddy, don't ride. Sliding around in the mud may be fun, but it damages trails, which ruins the fun for everyone. Use your head. If it's mushy, wait til it dries.

Bugs, thorny and/or poisonous plants, snakes and other manner of crawling critters—all these things are very real dangers on many Texas trails. It's always better to know what you're in for and be prepared for any eventuality.

Also, be very conscious of the temperature and the amount of sun you're being exposed to. When you're riding, you're sweating, whether it feels like it or not. In a climate as dry as it is in most of this state, the sweat can evaporate so fast from the surface of your skin that you don't even feel it. But you're still losing moisture, and it has to be replaced. Even breathing heavily through your mouth, as you will do on just about every ride, causes your body to lose precious fluids. Bring along plenty of water, and it's not a bad idea to carry a sports drink as well to keep your electrolytes up. I usually stick an energy bar in my pocket, regardless of the length of the ride I'm doing. Even if I don't need it, there's always a chance someone else will.

In addition to food and water, I carry an assortment of tools and other essentials in a seat pack, hydration pack, or a pocket. I always have a spare inner tube, a patch kit, and either a pump or a CO_2 dispenser. Tire levers

Leaving the lake road on the West Loop at Lake Bryan. Cheers to BVMBA and their trail-building efforts on this one.

and a chain tool come in handy, too. A multitool with Allen wrenches, screwdrivers, and a spoke wrench is also part of the standard gear. With these things, you are pretty much self-sufficient—as long as you know how to use them. If you're going out for more than a mile or two, you should know how to change a flat tire and adjust your brakes, at the very least. Any skills you acquire in bike mechanics only work to your advantage, so take a close look at how that bike works.

If you're lucky, riding a bike will change your life. It's more than a way to get from one place to another. It's more than exercise, and it's more than a sport. Spending a day on a mountain bike surrounded by trees, friends, and sky is one of the best things you can do for yourself and for the people in your life. Riding a bike regularly keeps you healthy and happy, looking and feeling good. It gives you time to push the clutter out of your mind and get your head straightened out from whatever the workweek crams in there. It can be thoughtful or thoughtless, meditative or purgative, pacifying or energizing. Riding a bike, you get in tune with your body in a way that few other pursuits allow or require. Most of all, mountain biking is fun—a lot of fun. And the more you explore the great state of Texas, the more you'll come to understand all the reasons we bikers do what we do.

So get out there and ride.

How to Use This Guide

Mountain Biking Texas describes fifty mountain bike rides in their entirety, as well as nine honorable mentions. Many of the featured rides are loops, beginning and ending at the same point but coming and going on different trails.

The difficulty of a loop may change dramatically depending on which direction you ride around the loop. If you are unfamiliar with the rides in this book, try them first as described here. The directions follow the path of least resistance and most fun (which does not necessarily mean easy). After you've been over the terrain, you can determine whether a given loop would be fun—or even feasible—in the reverse direction. Some trails are designated as one-way, so you don't have a choice.

Each ride description follows the same format:

Ride number: Number of the ride, relative to the rest of the rides in this book, with respect to their order of appearance.

Trail name: What the sign at the trailhead says, what the locals call it, or the name of the place surrounding it.

Location: The name of the town, the nearest town, or the park in which the trail lies.

Distance: Miles traveled from start to finish, mostly laid out in loops or out-and-back trips. Most of these numbers would be different with each trip around each trail, as one ride is never exactly the same as the one before. This provides a ballpark figure so that you know approximately what you're in for when you leave the trailhead behind.

Time: The time it took to move from the starting point to the ending point, usually the same place but not always. I didn't include time spent during any major transgressions from the route described, of which there were plenty. The time of these rides is gauged by my own riding speed, which I like to refer to as solidly intermediate. Some of you will be faster, and some of you will be slower. This is a general figure so that, again, you have an idea of what to expect.

Tread: The trail's surface, whether it's singletrack, doubletrack, jeep road, gravel path, etc. There are no rides here with a majority of paved surface, though some do have paved sections. Singletrack is first and foremost in desirability for any mountain biker, but plenty of trails in this book have doubletrack and jeep road that offer some great riding.

Aerobic level: The amount of hurt a trail will put on your heart and lungs, rated Easy, Moderate, or Strenuous. Distance, overall elevation gains, trail surface, and steepness of pitch were all considered when rating the aerobic level of each trail, but perhaps the biggest factor in this category will be the speed and consistency with which you, the individual riders, greet each ride. Your best bet is to ride at a pace where you feel most comfortable. With a few notable exceptions, the trails in this book should be accessible to most people with a bit of off-road biking experience.

Technical difficulty: The level of bike-handling skills required to ride a trail. These skills include climbing loose surfaces, climbing steep grades, descending both of these, dropping off rock ledges, and managing small obstacles like rocks, roots, logs, and any of the other things that can come at you during the course of a ride. The ratings are 1 to 5, with 5 being the most difficult. In rating these trails I used a Rails to Trails, like Lake Mineral Wells, as a 1 and the Emma Long trail as a 5. There are only a couple 5's here (Emma Long and Kelly Creek), and both should be approached only by experienced riders—and then with caution.

Highlights: Major sights or attractions along the way, or just a brief explanation of what makes a particular trail special.

Land status: The trails in this book are all legal—or were last time I rode them. Most of them are on state park land, and the rest are national park, national forest, city park, or privately owned land. Fees apply in many cases, so you should always check on this before riding.

Maps: A list of maps that could help you along your ride. Often they're not necessary, but sometimes they are. It's always better to be prepared. I've included maps of my own here, usually adapted from existing park maps or topo maps. Some of them provide detail; others are little more than a blob in a shape that's congruent or similar to the shape of the trail it hopes to describe. I'm no cartographer, I'm just trying to point the way.

Access: Directions from the nearest significant point to the beginning of the trail. This listing and a decent Texas road map are all you need to find any trail in this book.

Notes on the trail: Any items of significant interest regarding the history, topography, layout, or state of the trail or the area. Sometimes this is an extension of the highlights section, and sometimes it even offers worthwhile information.

The ride: The detailed description of the ride. In most cases I've provided a point-to-point description of my progress along a trail, marking intersections and significant gains or losses in elevation. In some instances, point-to-point descriptions are absent. Most often this will be because the trail in question doesn't lend itself to this kind of documentation. One important thing to remember when mountain biking is to have a spirit of exploration. Not every trail is a loop. Backtracking is as inevitable as a wrong turn, and out-and-back trips are often necessary—and not necessarily bad. Reversing direction on a dirt trail often means a whole different ride.

Another reason for the lack of point-to-points, and for lengthier "Notes on the Trail" sections, is that, well, Texas is a big, big place. In the course of the few years I've spent charting and mapping rides for this book, I haven't always been able to spend as much time in some places as I'd have liked. Big Bend Ranch is one example of this. The park's sprawling network of barely used jeep roads beckons for weeks and months of examination from the saddle, far more than the couple trips of a few days that I was able to devote to it. In these cases, I have tried to offer as much detailed information as I can, along with directions to the trailheads and whatever knowledge I was able to gather on the trip. On many rides—as you'll see the more of the state you explore—you'd be well advised to carry a compass. And it also helps to remember that getting lost is sometimes part of the process and can also be the most memorable part of a trip. So enjoy it, and don't stress every wrong turn.

Lastly, the **Honorable Mentions** at the end of each region in the book detail the rides that didn't make the cut as a full-featured route. In many cases it's not because they aren't great rides; rather it's because they're overcrowded, environmentally sensitive to heavy traffic, or just severely out of the way. Be sure to read through these. A jewel might be lurking among them—and you might have some suggestions of your own for future editions.

Rules of the Trail

If every mountain biker always yielded the right-of-way, stayed on the trail, avoided wet or muddy trails, never cut switchbacks, always rode in control, showed respect for other trail users, and carried out every last scrap of what was carried in (candy wrappers and bike-part debris included)—in short, if we all did the right things—we wouldn't need a list of rules governing our behavior.

The fact is, most mountain bikers *are* conscientious and are trying to do the right thing; however, thousands of miles of dirt trails have been closed due to the irresponsible habits of a few riders.

Here are some basic guidelines adapted from the International Mountain Bicycling Association Rules of the Trail. These guidelines can help prevent damage to land, water, plants, and wildlife; maintain trail access; and avoid conflicts with other backcountry visitors and trail users.

1. Only ride on trails that are open. Don't trespass on private land, and be sure to obtain any necessary permits. If you're not sure if a trail is closed or if you need a permit, don't hesitate to ask.

2. Keep your bicycle under control. Watch the condition of the trail at all times, and follow the appropriate speed regulations and recommendations.

3. Yield to others on the trail. Make your approach well known in advance, either with a friendly greeting or a bell. When approaching a corner, junction, or blind spot, expect to encounter other trail users. When passing others, show your respect by slowing to a walking pace.

4. Don't startle animals. Animals may be easily scared by sudden approaches or loud noises. For your safety—and the safety of others in the area as well as the animals themselves—give all wildlife a wide berth. When encountering horses, defer to the horseback riders' directions.

5. Practice zero impact. Be aware of the impact you're making on the trail beneath you. You should not ride under conditions where you will leave evidence of your passing, such as on certain soils after rain. If a ride features optional side hikes into wilderness areas, be a zero-impact hiker, too. Whether you're on bike or on foot, stick to existing trails, leave gates as you found them, and carry out everything you brought in.

6. Be prepared. Know the equipment you are using, the area where you'll be riding, and your cycling abilities and limitations. Avoid unnecessary breakdowns by keeping your equipment in good shape. When you head out, bring spare parts and supplies for weather changes. Be sure to wear appropriate safety gear, including a helmet, and learn how to be self-sufficient.

West Texas

Anyone who tells you there are no mountains in Texas hasn't spent much time west of the Pecos. From the Franklin Mountains in the farthest corner of the state to the Sierra del Carmen in the Big Bend—not to mention the Christmas and Glass Mountains lying between them—there's plenty of elevation to be gained (and lost!) in this history- and activity-rich portion of the Lone Star State. This is Texas at its biggest and best, its most beautiful and its most dangerous.

Many of the rides included in this section are inside the boundaries of Big Bend National Park. You'll also notice that they're all on dirt roads. That's because bikes are allowed to go only where a car can go inside the park. Disappointing, sure, but spend any amount of time hiking the trails inside the park and you'll likely agree that these paths are better left to boots and boots alone. Besides, the primitive roads open up more miles of riding, surrounded by the most awe-inspiring scenery that Texas has to offer, than most mortals could cover in a lifetime. (Sounds like a challenge, doesn't it?)

West of the national park, the towns of Terlingua and Lajitas are both home to some killer trails; unfortunately most of them are on private land. Locals and the guide and tour shops they work for are your best bets at gaining access to these rides—a definite possibility if you've got some time—but don't try them on your own. Landowners in this state don't appreciate unannounced and unwelcome guests, so as with *any* private land in Texas, get permission first.

A bit farther west down FM 170 (perhaps the most scenic drive in the state) is the relatively new Big Bend Ranch State Park. You want primitive? Here it is. Again, biking is limited to those places accessible by car—except for organized tours to El Solitario—but this place is criminally undervisited and the odds of your having the entire park to yourself are good. These old ranch roads can keep you spinning for hours, even days, if you've got the time and the energy to explore them.

If the land out here looks rough and rugged, that's because it is. Carry at least an extra tube, a pump, a patch kit, tools, a compass, and some food. Riding in the desert—this is the Chihuahuan Desert, extended up from Mexico—requires good preparation and extreme caution. Carry more water than you would normally consider. In this climate sweat evaporates before you can even feel it on your skin. You also lose lots of moisture just by breathing heavily. So without feeling a drop of sweat, you're well on your way to dehydration. And you never know when a wrong turn will mean an extra two hours in the sun and heat. Always wear sunscreen. No matter how fit you are, the sun out here can reduce you to a whimpering puddle if you're not prepared.

If the sun is mean from a distance, the local flora is downright nasty—and right under your feet. There are so many ways to get stabbed, stuck, pricked, and punctured that trying to explain it all here would be silly. Just remember: Everything here has a thorn. These plants have to defend themselves from the hungry and ever-thirsty desert wildlife, and they've developed some pretty amazing ways of doing that. Be careful. Look, don't touch.

This section also includes some rides in the not-so-western part of West Texas, in the Concho Valley and down near the Rio Grande near the Amistad Reservoir. These are scenic places all and well worth the trip.

If you haven't traveled to the western portion of the state, make time for a trip. I can guarantee that if you do, it won't be your last. The dust of West Texas has a way of getting under your skin, and the mountains stay clear in your mind long after the vacation is over and you're back at work, slogging away, dreaming about the bike.

Franklin Mountains
State Park Trail

Location: El Paso.

Distance: 15 miles.

Time: 2.5-hour loop.

Tread: Mostly singletrack, some doubletrack.

Aerobic level: Strenuous.

Technical difficulty: 4.

Highlights: There's some serious elevation out here in El Paso, and these are some serious trails. Beautiful views of the Franklin Mountains and a seemingly endless spread of open land make this a trail worthy of an all-day exploration.

Land status: State park.

Maps: Free park map at headquarters; USGS El Paso, North Franklin Mountains.

Access: Take I–10 west to the Canutillo/Trans-Mountain exit. Turn right, toward the mountains (there's a sign for the park). The park is 3.8 miles east of I–10—watch for the entrance sign; it's easy to miss. Drive through the main gate, pay your fee, grab a map, and head to the first parking lot on the left, marked MOUNTAIN BIKE TRAIL. There are rest rooms and shaded picnic tables here, and the trailhead is clearly marked.

Notes on the trail: The trails in Franklin Mountains State Park are outstanding. Long stretches of singletrack that pierce the horizon and roll over the lower reaches of the surprisingly scenic Franklin range offer fine technical riding as well as some gradually graded and really speedy stuff. Tight switchbacks, rocky drops, easy ups and downs, and some very rewarding climbs add up to just about everything you could ask for in a trail.

There are plenty more trails to ride in the immediate area, but land status precludes me from mentioning them here. According to the locals there's no question of illegality, it's just not public land. Stop in at Crazy

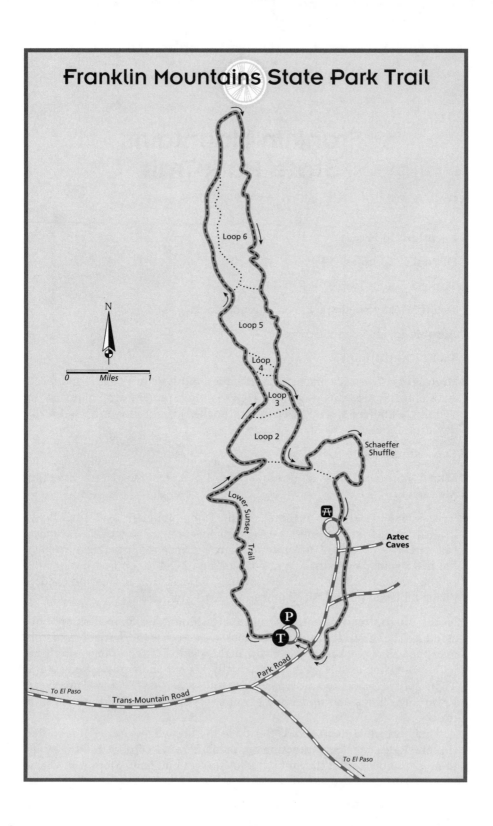

Franklin Mountains State Park Trail

N

0 Miles 1

Loop 6

Loop 5

Loop 4

Loop 3

Loop 2

Schaeffer Shuffle

Lower Sunset Trail

Aztec Caves

P

T

Park Road

Trans-Mountain Road

To El Paso

To El Paso

Your author, awed by the mountains of El Paso.

Cat Bicycles and work the shop guys for info. They're only too happy to oblige, and they may even invite you along for a ride.

The Ride

0.0 Lower Sunset trailhead. Shortly after you take off, the beginner's trail branches off to the left. This is a narrow and extremely smooth path that winds out and back to the main trail at 0.3 mile. Stay left at the split immediately following the connection.

1.2 After diving through a couple gulleys, a long, gradual downhill brings you to a sharp right downward turn and a couple of hairy switchbacks. Careful. Now the trail begins a series of nice ups and downs, following the contours of the edge of the mountains.

2.6 Rugged terrain and steep drops are the norm at this point. The longer downhills will have you whooping with glee. Don't hold back—let it out!

3.1 A really long downhill brings you to the edge of a ridge. Ride along this ridge for a short while until you hit some switchbacks and start the climb back out.

3.8 A sign reading BMBA points to the left; follow it. The other way cuts across to the return route for an easy out if you've had enough. But, of course, you haven't—so go left, power through the gravel creekbed, and come out the other side.

4.3 Here's another connector trail going off to the right. A long, gradual climb follows. The relief of the terrain is less drastic out here than at the beginning, the hills more rolling, and the trail smoother.

5.7 A shortcut points due east and marks the outermost point of the smaller, 11-mile loop. The main path keeps going to the left, heading out into the seemingly endless distance. The trail leads down into the creekbed for a brief gravelly stint and then climbs back out of it on the right.

6.7 Another shortcut leading off the main trail to the right, this one marked with the number 19. From here the terrain flattens out a bit, with more gradual hills and sharp corners.

7.6 A turnoff from the main trail leads to some narrow singletrack. Turning off here means missing one of the shortcuts, but if you're going the distance this is worth it.

8.7 The trail dumps out to the right and bends back toward the beginning. Doubletrack leading to the northwest brings you to where the numbered markers start in reverse.

10.2 The first mile or so of the return trail is calm, flat terrain—beautiful scenery with a great use of the contour of the land. Just after the 10-mile point, you'll begin a gradual climb, then a nice downhill, where you should watch the corners—the ground is a bit slippy until you get used to it.

11.1 Here you start passing the shortcut signs, which are pointed the other direction on this side as well, indicating that the trail is not one-way. On this side, the trail skirts the very edge of the mountains.

13.5 Passing Sign 42 the trail comes to a T. Turn left to get to the Schaeffer Shuffle extension and the Aztec Caves, or go right to return to the beginning of the trail. (*Note:* At the time of writing, Schaeffer Shuffle was being worked on, and the return trail up the hill and running along the east side of the park road was not yet complete. It should be finished and marked by the time you read this, though. Schaeffer Shuffle is a tight and steep loop added on just below the Aztec Caves camping area.)

14.1 The climb up to Aztec Caves is a true grunt, just about a mile long and about 400 feet of gain. You'll pass the nature trail on the way up, but that's foot traffic only. Up past the parking lot is where you'll catch the upper trail back to the parking area. The road leads back to it as well.

15.6 Parking area.

Oso Loop

Location: Big Bend Ranch State Park.

Distance: 12-mile loop.

Time: 2.5 hours.

Tread: Unimproved jeep roads and doubletrack.

Aerobic level: Moderate.

Technical difficulty: 2.

Highlights: Jeep roads aren't the most thrilling mountain biking terrain in the world, but, as with anywhere in this beautiful park, the scenery is what you're here for. There's no shortage of amazing desert views along this ride.

Land status: State park.

Maps: Free park map; USGS Agua Adentro Mountain.

Access: From Presidio, take FM 170 east to Casa Piedra Road (FM 169) and turn left. Follow this road for 7 miles, and then turn right on the main park road. After 2.4 miles, there is a gate—be sure to get the combination from park headquarters before setting out. After that it's about 13 miles to the Papalotito Colorado campsites, where you'll park for this ride. From there, head back west on the main road until you reach the Oso Loop.

Notes on the trail: While there are many offshoots and wrong turns to be made along this route, following the USGS quad will keep you on the right track. Don't head *too* far south. And keep an eye out for the campsites along the trail—their absence for too long will let you know you're going the wrong way (yes, this is from experience). But, as with any activity in the Big Bend Ranch, the scenery and the solitude are worth any trouble you might have.

The Ride

   0.0   From the Papalotito Colorado parking area, head back out to the main road and turn right, going back the way you came in. The main road offers a great ride in itself, taking in the mountain

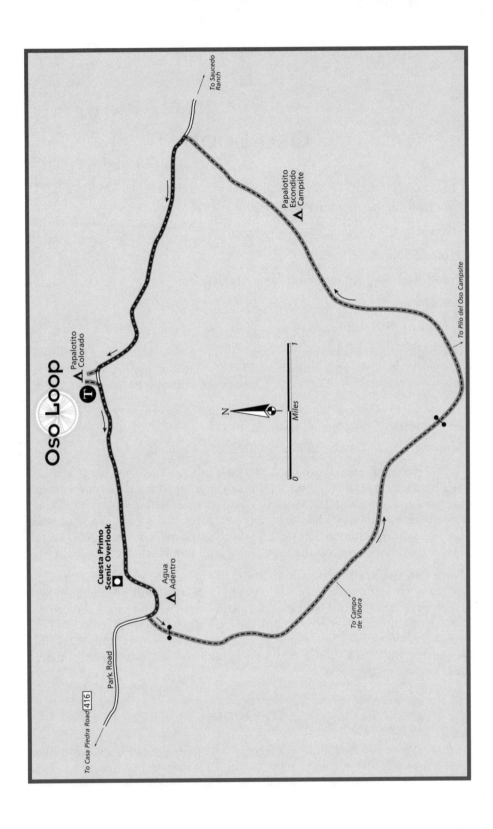

views and the desert flora and an occasional glimpse of the park's roaming herd of Texas longhorns.

2.2 Turn left at the OSO LOOP sign to begin the jeep road portion of the ride. Right after the sign for Agua Adentro, the road is blocked by a gate—or at least it was when I was out here—and there were longhorns everywhere. This is a ranch, after all, so don't be afraid to cross a cattleguard or open a gate—as long as it's not locked—just close it behind you.

3.8 At the first big fork in the road, keep to the inside, taking the path up and over a small ridge to hug the contour of the hillside. Use that as a general rule all along this loop—keeping to the inside—and you shouldn't go too far wrong. It's the seemingly innocent intersections that can have you suddenly 5 miles offtrack to the south that you have to watch out for. Stay to the left—and be prepared to climb a bit.

4.6 You can tell that a lot of cattle spend a lot of time in this spot. Roll through, past the big blue barrel, watching out for the big brown cow-pies, and up the wash on the other side.

4.8 Here's the bottom of a pretty imposing-looking climb. The terrain is loose and rocky, so this is indeed a tough one, but it's short, too. At the top you'll pass through another gate marked with the geometric longhorn head you'll see throughout the ranch—a welcome sign that you are not lost. The road down from here is a long, shaky, loose downhill that's fun and slightly treacherous. Watch your speed.

5.9 Just past another cattle tank is the Pilo del Oso campsite. The trail turns sharply northward here, heading across a ridge, and you can get a good view of the lovely downhills that await you.

6.2 A nice long downhill, steady enough to build up some good speed, leads you past a pair of turnoffs, one closed and the other ungated and heading off to the right. The open one with its distant rock structures looks pretty inviting for exploration. Keep straight, though. The speedy fun continues after a short climb.

6.8 Solid, rocky doubletrack surface makes the descents fast and the climbing easier than on the first half of the loop. Hit the uphills in a big gear and you're at the top before you even feel it.

7.4 At the top of this climb you can see Sauceda Ranch off to the east, part of a stunningly beautiful panoramic view.

7.5 Papalotito Escondido campsite, up on a plateau, has a gorgeous 360-degree view. From here the road turns into another long, fast descent that crosses a creek and flattens out a little bit at the bottom.

8.1 Back at the main road, turn left and head back toward Papalotito Colorado, where you parked. The road has some nice up- and downhills along the way, as well as plenty of big chunks of rock for your pinch-flat pleasure, so don't go to sleep just yet.

10.3 Papalotito Colorado campsite parking area.

Old Maverick Road

Location: Big Bend National Park.

Distance: 12.6 miles one-way.

Time: 1.5 hours.

Tread: Improved jeep road.

Aerobic level: Moderate.

Technical difficulty: 1.

Highlights: As with any ride in Big Bend National Park, the draw here is the scenery and the chance to view it from the seat of a bicycle. In springtime this ride is absolutely stunning, the desert floor carpeted with wildflowers and the Rattlesnake Mountains looming dry and forbidding to the west.

Land status: National Park.

Maps: Free park map; Trails Illustrated Big Bend topo map; USGS Terlingua and Castolon.

Access: From U.S. 90 in Marathon, go south on U.S. 385 into Big Bend National Park. At Panther Junction turn right and follow TX 118 almost to the Maverick entrance station on the west end of the park. Just before the station there's a sign for the Old Maverick Road on the left. Here's where you start.

Notes on the trail: This one's more a road than a trail, really, but it's too rough for a road bike and too beautiful to see from inside a car. The wide gravel road is a pretty decent surface for the most part. It's raked fairly smooth and host to enough traffic to keep too much big stuff from accumulating, though the inevitable washboards will get you shaking sooner or later.

I did this one north to south, ending at the junction with the Ross Maxwell Scenic Drive at its end near Santa Elena Canyon. This is a good place to have a ride waiting if you can swing it. If not, the elevation going back north isn't *too* bad. Just make sure you bring plenty of water—a Camelback is a must for doing this both ways, as is an energy bar or two.

Old Maverick Road

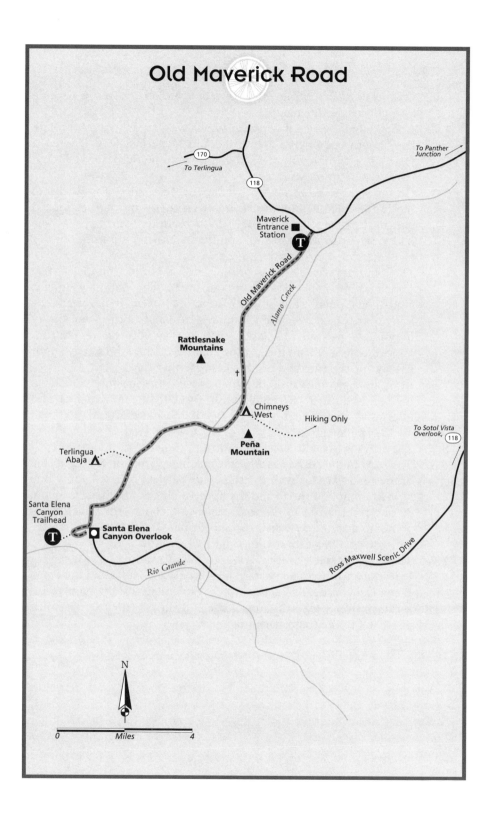

The Ride

0.0   Trailhead, near the Maverick entrance station. There's a parking lot right inside the gate.

1.7   A long, gentle descent gets you under way, carrying you through the smooth opening stretch of the Old Maverick Road. There's a little bit of climbing to do as you approach the Rattlesnake Mountains, rising up on your right.

3.0   On the right side, an unimproved dirt road leads to the west into the Rattlesnake Mountains. I didn't go there, but it sure looked enticing. After rolling through these foothills, you begin a nice long descent away from the mountains, passing a number of dry creeks and some roadside gravesites along the way.

6.1   The Chimneys trailhead is on the left, as is the Chimneys West campsite. Luna's Jacal is in this same area. The Chimneys hike is a gorgeous, mostly flat desert hike to a group of rock formations known as, of course, the Chimneys, which feature some pretty impressive petroglyphs (and some not so impressive graffiti). Unfortunately, it's no bikes allowed. You might want to save your energy for the ride and do this hike another day.

7.3   After an easy creek crossing the surface turns to some wonderful hard-packed dirt, careening west through some flatlands and offering a spectacular view of the Rattlesnake Mountains from another perspective.

8.7   The surface turns to washboard again, though not for too long.

9.9   The road to the Terlingua Abaja campsite appears on the right side of the road here, as well as an incredible view of a red and white striped mountain range and the approaching Santa Elena Canyon.

11.3   A long right curve in the road leads to a sharp left, which takes you onto a seriously washboarded surface. It doesn't last, though, and you're almost there. Stop and look around.

12.6   The Ross Maxwell Scenic Drive. If you're heading back north for the return trip by bike, take a short break and check out the Santa Elena Canyon overlook, just up the pavement a bit. If you've got a ride waiting, take this road east and then north past Castolon and back to the main park road.

4

Glenn Spring Loop

Location: Big Bend National Park.

Distance: 28-mile loop.

Time: 3 hours.

Tread: Jeep road, some improved and some not so improved.

Aerobic level: Moderate to strenuous.

Technical difficulty: 2.

Highlights: This long, lonely trek through the eastern foothills of the Chisos Mountains is a good way to cover a lot of miles in the park without too rough a ride. The loop stays on good roads and is exposed at all times to breathtaking scenery. The ruins of the Mariscal Mine, a small cemetery, and a few backcountry campsites are landmarks and provide rest stops along the way.

Land status: National Park.

Maps: Free park map; Trails Illustrated Big Bend topo map; USGS Glenn Spring, San Vicente, and Solis.

Access: From U.S. 90 in Marathon, go south on U.S. 385 into Big Bend National Park. At Panther Junction turn left and follow TX 118 for about 5 miles to the turnoff for Glenn Spring Road. Take this about 8 miles to the junction of Glenn Spring and Black Gap Roads. The loop described here will start out Black Gap Road to the southwest.

Notes on the trail: You could start this loop from the main park road at the Glenn Spring Road turnoff, which would add about 16 miles of dirt riding to your trip. This would be a wise choice if you don't have a 4x4 vehicle; there are a couple stretches of pretty rough going between the park road and Black Gap Road.

    With only a few exceptions—one of them being a veritable wall of rock that would take Hans Rey with very sticky tires to get up—the surface is a decent one, improved gravel road wide enough for two cars to pass each other. There are washboarded sections, of course, and some deep and sandy gravel parts that take some huffing and puffing to get through. But mostly it's pleasant going on gradual grades. And the scenery is nothing

Glenn Spring Loop

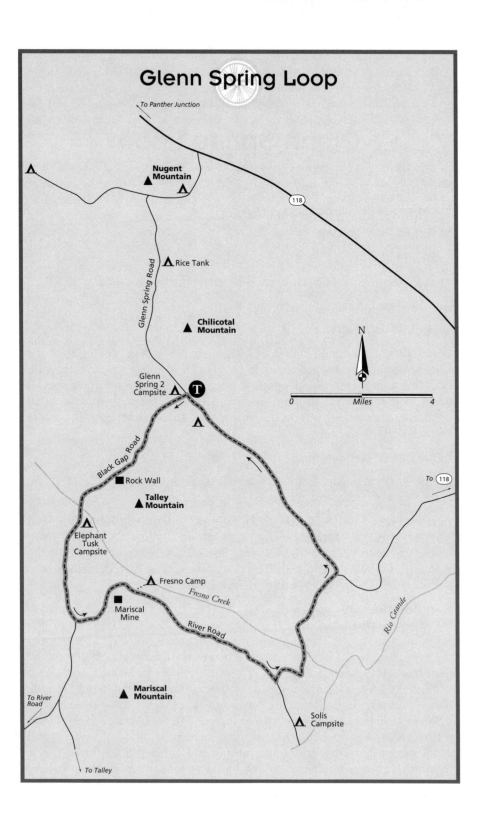

To Panther Junction

Nugent
Mountain

118

Rice Tank

Glenn Spring Road

Chilicotal
Mountain

N

0   Miles   4

Glenn
Spring 2
Campsite

T

Black Gap Road

Rock Wall

Talley
Mountain

To 118

Elephant
Tusk
Campsite

Fresno Camp

Fresno Creek

Mariscal
Mine

River Road

Rio Grande

Mariscal
Mountain

To River
Road

Solis
Campsite

To Talley

short of majestic and spectacular, the Chisos looming to the northwest, Talley Mountain the near-constant center of your loop, and lots of ridges and creekbeds and other distant ranges along the way. Bring a camera.

Though it's not *technically* demanding, this loop still demands plenty of your legs and lungs, so attempt it only if you're up for a long time in the saddle. Pack a lunch and bring plenty of water, too; there are so many nice places to stop, it'd be a shame to just blow by them all.

Caution: This trail does get pretty close to the Rio Grande, which also means it gets pretty close to the U.S.-Mexico border. Not to be alarmist, but there are frequent reports of trouble near the border, especially on the eastern end of the park, about unattended vehicles being broken into and of people disappearing. Reports of the former are fact, the latter mostly hearsay; regardless, be careful. Watch your stuff, and keep an eye behind you. Awareness is the key to staying safe in any situation.

The Ride

0.0   Junction of Glenn Spring and Black Gap Roads. Head out to the southwest on Black Gap Road.

1.0   The road takes a downward turn into a wide valley, with the Chisos Mountains jutting up from the desert floor directly ahead of you. There are a couple of pretty tricky drops on the way down that hill, tight and rocky stuff that requires attention.

2.0   Some low, rolling hills and a good surface keep you moving pretty well. A couple of easy creek crossings pop up along the way, but mostly it's steady riding through this part.

4.0   Suddenly, a sheer wall of rock blocks your way like some gigantic upended concrete shelf. A pile of smaller rocks at the bottom is an attempt at a ramp. You can walk up it, though. There's a steady climb for a while on the other side.

5.2   Cross Fresno Creek. There was actually a good bit of water when I rode here.

5.3   Reach the Elephant Tusk Trail junction. The campsite is on your left and the trail on your right. This trail is open to hikers and horses, but you and your bike will have to stick to the road.

7.0   That squat-looking mountain poking above the ridge off in the distance to your right is called Cow Heaven Mountain. How cool is that?

8.8   River Road Junction. Turn left here. Though the surface looks good, it's not too far before you hit some sand that puts a serious drag on your momentum. Keep moving; it stays this way for a little less than a mile.

9.5   Cresting a sandy climb, which is not much fun, you meet a much better surface, washboarded though it is, for the trip back down this hill.

Is there anyplace more beautiful than the middle of nowhere?

10.8   Here's where I got a flat tire.

11.4   Arrive at the ruins of the Mariscal Mine—a small series of low, crumbled structures that used to be a productive mine of cinnabar ore, which is mined for quicksilver, or mercury. The mine opened at the turn of the twentieth century and had its heyday from 1916 to the mid-1920s. It was operational again shortly after World War II, but profitability quickly fell off and the mine closed.

11.5   The Fresno Camp appears here on your left, a beautiful little spot close to the mine's ruins.

14.7   Long stretches of washboard road might shake a few fillings loose through the section just after the camp. Keep on; it doesn't last forever.

15.6   After heading down a long way through some nasty, mushy gravel, the road suddenly turns to hard-packed dirt. After the other, it feels like riding on a cloud. And as it's still downhill, it's no problem bringing your speed up to 25 mph or so. Quite a blast!

16.7   The road to the Solis campsite is on the right. Here the trail bends back to the north away from the Rio Grande, which is just out of sight up ahead. This wide floodplain is a perfect spot to stop for a break.

17.6 The trail starts rising gradually for the climb back to the beginning, but the surface is good and the going is easy, for now.

20.0 The hardpack turns to somewhat soft dirt, which is not so bad. Along the way you'll drop into some small ravines and creek valleys, but for the most part it's steady, easy climbing.

20.8 Here's the junction of River and Glenn Spring Roads. Turn left onto Glenn Spring Road for the home stretch.

21.4 Gravel; deep, slow gravel. It'll last about a mile or so, some of it on tough climbs.

23.0 The surface improves, and you keep climbing steadily.

26.0 More of the same: climbing, decent surface, and Talley Mountain approaching again on your left.

27.4 The Glenn Spring 2 campsite looks like a good place to spend some time—gorgeous views.

28.0 Junction of Glenn Spring and Black Gap Roads. If you parked here, you're done. If you parked at the main road, keep to the right and follow Glenn Spring Road another 8 miles out to the park road.

Old Ore Road

Location: Big Bend National Park.

Distance: 29 miles one-way.

Time: 3 hours.

Tread: Unimproved jeep road.

Aerobic level: Strenuous.

Technical difficulty: 2.

Highlights: Though it's the toughest Big Bend ride in this book, it's also one of the most peaceful and beautiful spots in the park. Visitation is lower in this area than it is near the popular places like the Basin and Santa Elena Canyon. You'll likely see at least a few people down near Rio Grande Village, but that might even be a welcome sight at the end of the ride. You should also take note of the various campsites and the road conditions and distances to them, because you'll definitely want to return to at least a couple of them to spend a night or two.

Old Ore Road

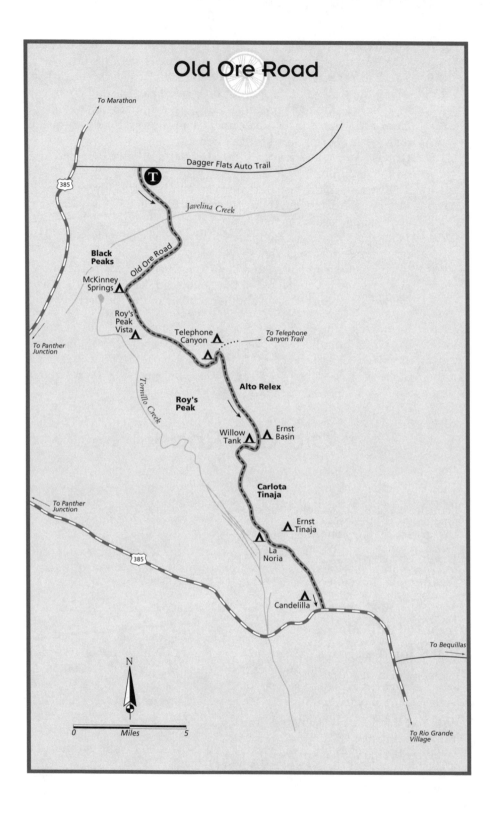

To Marathon

Dagger Flats Auto Trail

385

Javelina Creek

Black Peaks

Old Ore Road

McKinney
Springs

Roy's
Peak
Vista

Telephone
Canyon

To Telephone
Canyon Trail

To Panther
Junction

Tornillo Creek

**Roy's
Peak**

Alto Relex

Willow
Tank

Ernst
Basin

**Carlota
Tinaja**

To Panther
Junction

385

Ernst
Tinaja

La
Noria

Candelilla

To Bequillas

N

0   Miles   5

To Rio Grande
Village

Land status: National Park.

Maps: Free park map; Trails Illustrated Big Bend topo map; USGS McKinney Springs, Roy's Peak, and San Vicente.

Access: From U.S. 90 in Marathon, go south on U.S. 385 into Big Bend National Park. Turn left onto the Dagger Flats Auto Trail and go about 2 miles to Old Ore Road, which will head south.

Notes on the trail: By far your best bet is to get dropped off at the northern end of Old Ore Road on Dagger Flats and have a ride waiting for you at the southern end, near Rio Grande Village. If you have to do this ride as an out-and-back, remember that there's an overall elevation gain going south to north. You might want to start at the southern end and leave the "easier" part for the second half of the ride. This way, you end near the hot springs, which you'll most likely need after a full day on the bike. Start early, because it'll take you most of a day.

As you ride, consider this road's utilitarian past. Back in the early portion of the last century, the Old Ore Road was used to haul the quicksilver mined down in the Mariscal Mine up to Marathon, about 50 miles north of the park's entrance. The history runs deep out here, from the running off of the Chisos Indians by the Mescalero Apaches to the running off of the Apaches by the Comanche. The Comanche controlled the territory from here on up to Oklahoma and used Big Bend as a passage to Mexico, which they also raided relentlessly for the better part of a century. Pancho Villa raided settlements here until the U.S. Cavalry chased him off. Ranching came later, erecting fences and drastically altering the ecosystem from grassland to the scrub desert it remains today.

It goes without saying that you should have more water than you'll need when you embark on this ride. Your body loses plenty of the precious liquid even if you don't feel like you're sweating, and you never know when a mechanical malfunction (or a wipeout) can keep you out here far longer than you'd planned. Watch yourself and your stuff as you approach the southern part of the trail; it's pretty close to the U.S.-Mexico border and people's stuff (not to mention people themselves) have been known to disappear.

The Ride

0.0   Depart Dagger Flats and head south on the Old Ore Road. It's nice, flat, fairly easy going at the outset, a high ridge separating you from the Sierra del Caballo Muerto, or Dead Horse Mountains, off in the distance to the east.

3.8   Cross Javelina Creek, which was dry when I rode but certainly looked like it could carry some water in wetter days.

5.0   The trail takes a turn upward, climbing on a decent surface and a decent grade up and over a bit of that ridge you've been seeing off to your left. The trail heads back downward after this brief climb, crossing a couple additional creekbeds and then sweeping westward, offering some great views of the Black Peaks.

9.8 The McKinney Springs campsite is on your left here, which itself is close to McKinney Springs, a water-bearing natural spring. This area was settled by the McKinneys, who found their fortune in quicksilver mining. Avoid taking the water if you can; the local fauna have it tough enough finding consistent water supplies without competing with the likes of us.

11.9 Slightly sandy road threads between a couple of low peaks on the way to this turnoff for the Roy's Peak Vista campsite. Both these sites are superb places to pass some time, but save that for another day, as there's still a long way to go.

13.4 The road skirts closely to the edge of a ridge here, passing next to Roy's Peak on the right. The surface can be mushy, but for the most part it keeps you moving just fine.

15.2 A sharp set of turns in the trail takes you between a pair of campsites along some sandy road, so pedal hard through the drop and pop up the other side. The way splits here, with a left taking you to the campsites and a right sending you on your way. These are the Telephone Canyon campsites, which sit at the end of an extension of the Telephone Canyon Trail—a remote and rugged hike through the Dead Horse Mountains and the Ernst Valley.

16.1 There's a bit of climbing to do now as you roll up and over the edge of the Alto Relex, a steep ridge on the edge of the mountains. Though the surface gets a bit sketchy through here, trudge on, as the downhill gets smooth and fast and carries you quite a ways with little effort.

19.0 Passing between the Ernst Basin campsite on the left and the Willow Tank campsite on the right, the road gets a bit loose and shaky, passing over a few small ridges in a westward bend before continuing the southward descent. A spring somewhere east of the road feeds a skinny creek, which you have to cross.

22.8 A long, flat run brings you to a ridgeline overlooking the wide bed of Tornillo Creek. There's water down here, too—or at least there was at one time and no doubt will be again. Carlota Tinaja is just to the left of the trail, which takes some strange twists, dropping and climbing quickly through both loose rock and solid gravel.

25.1 At this point, as you ride past the La Noria campsite and La Noria cemetery, you may very well start seeing other park visitors. Just on the edge of Tornillo Creek, the ruins of La Noria village draw many carbound day hikers out to look around. Just south of here is the turnoff to the Ernst Tinaja campsite, another popular auto destination.

25.3 The turnoff to the Telephone Canyon Trail, which heads back north. It's a straight, fairly flat and sandy shot down to the park road from here. Watch out for auto traffic—it doesn't always watch out for you.

29.0   On the right is the turnoff to the Candelilla campsite. If you have to ride the return trip and don't need to visit Rio Grande Village for anything, this might be a good place to rest before starting up again. It'll save you the sandy climb back from the main road.

29.3   The main park road. Take a left to ride the road to Rio Grande Village.

Devil's River
State Natural Area Trail

Location: Val Verde County, north of Del Rio.

Distance: 12.5-mile loop.

Time: 2 hours.

Tread: Mostly dirt doubletrack; part wide gravel road.

Aerobic level: Moderate.

Technical difficulty: 3.

Highlights: Great Hill Country views, fantastic bird-watching, and very little traffic make this isolated park a great weekend destination. The trail, except for a few pretty hairy spots, is a relatively easy one, made somewhat demanding by two points of fairly extreme elevation change—which you can walk, if you must.

Land status: State Natural Area, maintained by TPWD; fees apply.

Maps: Free topo map from park; USGS Dolan Springs.

Access: From Del Rio, go north on TX 277 for 43 miles to a dirt road on your left called Dolan Creek Road. Turn left and follow this 22 miles to park headquarters. The dirt road within the park makes up the lower portion of the trail, so you can start anywhere along the road.

Notes on the trail: If you're looking to get away from it all, Devil's River State Natural Area is one of the most remote-feeling parks I've encountered

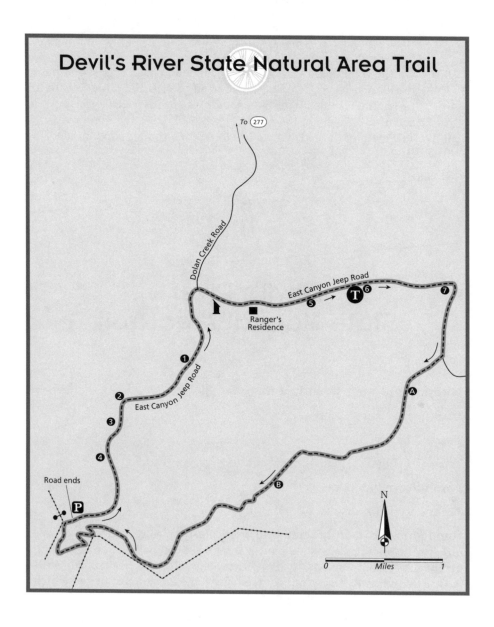

Devil's River State Natural Area Trail

To (277)

Dolan Creek Road

East Canyon Jeep Road

⑤ →

T ⑥ →

⑦

Ranger's
Residence

①

East Canyon Jeep Road

②

❸

❹

Road ends

P

Ⓐ

Ⓑ

N

0   Miles   1

in Texas, separated from the middle of nowhere by a 22-mile dirt road. The trail, which spans some of the highest and lowest reaches of the park's acreage, is a combination of the wide, gravel park road and a former jeep road that's grown over into doubletrack. This is Hill Country scenery at its finest and most rugged—outside the abundant live oaks, pretty much everything has a thorn or two on it. Visitation to the park is limited, so reservations are usually necessary. As I was stationed at campsite #6, about 2 miles east of headquarters, that's where the ride begins.

The Ride

0.0 Campsite #6. From here I headed east, toward campsite #7, riding the loop in a clockwise direction. The first mile or so of the park road is a nice ride, rolling up and down between 1,600 and 1,700 feet. No big climbs, until . . .

1.3 This is the big hill the ranger warned me about when I registered. It'll come into view after you pass campsite #7, and you'll want to be sure that your cycling shoes are also made for walking. It's almost 250 feet of elevation gain in a *very* short distance here, but when you get to the top, you stay at the top.

1.5 The hill planes out a tiny bit, but it keeps climbing for another quarter mile or so. Turn around and look behind you—the road disappears downward, and the view is worth the grunt to get up here.

1.7 The road bends to the left, and the trail breaks off to the right, by the hike/bike symbols sign. The trail starts out a wide, smooth jeep road lined with prickly pear, with stunning views of the folded terrain of East Canyon on the right and Rough Spring Canyon on the left.

2.4 The surface stays smooth and the terrain flat for a while. Another hike/bike sign here points you straight as the main jeep trail banks left. Here it becomes packed-dirt doubletrack, winding through a couple of gates and thick foliage that grows ever closer to the legs.

2.7 Backcountry campsite A, in an open meadow with a beautiful view.

3.7 You'll head gradually downhill for a while, though you'll still be on the high ground between the canyons. Past another hike/bike sign, the trail opens up into another meadow.

4.1 Backcountry campsite B, in another flat, open spot with a great view. Here the trail is a bit less clearly marked, but wherever the route is obscured, small rock cairns show the way.

4.5 Another hike/bike sign.

5.0 The trail bends through a gate to the left, past a small windmill, and through some sections that, when I rode here, were so overgrown with cactus that I had to carry the bike through. Watch the feet and ankles—there are some long thorns out here.

5.8 At this point you'll head off the high ground and begin the trip down more than 400 feet to the park road. A sharp downward turn makes for one of the nastier parts of the trail, and as the path becomes more obscure and you find yourself walking a bit more than you may have bargained for, stop and take a look around. The views are worth the trudgery. Keep an eye out for the cairns.

6.2 The hike/bike sign is a bit off the trail you're likely on, but that's OK; just keep along the fenceline and follow the signs. Careful, it's still pretty steep.

6.5 After a long drop you'll come up over a slight rise, and you'll be able to see the main road down below. Keep close watch for the trail markers. The downhill eases up a bit, and the trail becomes ridable and fun with some nice fast downhill stretches—though you'll want to keep your guard up, as steep, rocky sections pop up now and again.

6.9 The trail flattens out again, briefly, before taking the final plunge to near the level of Dolan Creek. Parts of this descent are loose and boulder-strewn, so keep your head up and your butt back on the way down.

7.1 The fenceline you've been following turns into a gate, which you'll pass through, riding on some gravel doubletrack until you hit the main road again.

7.3 Turn right on the main road. Though it may seem too soon to be leaving the trail behind, what with 5 miles left to go in the ride, the views of the canyon walls, the creek, and the surrounding hillsides ought to take care of any grievances about being out here on your bike. Get in the big ring and enjoy.

9.0 Campsite #3. The road is a bit washboarded, but the views are still outstanding.

9.6 Here you come to a bit of a climb, which leads past campsite #2 and to a cattleguard as the hill tops out.

10.0 Campsite #1, on more rolling hills and sheer canyon walls pocked with caves and holes.

10.8 Turn right at the intersection at the park's entrance with all the directional signs.

11.1 This is the late-arrival camping area, near park headquarters. Pass the headquarters building, climb a bit past the ranger's residence, and follow the road to the right toward campsites 5 through 7.

11.9 Campsite #5.

12.6 Campsite #6, where the ride began.

Rio Grande River Trail

Location: Seminole Canyon State Historical Park, near Comstock.

Distance: 6.6 miles round-trip.

Time: 1 hour.

Tread: Mostly doubletrack.

Aerobic level: Easy.

Technical difficulty: 2.

Highlights: The canyon views and the tremendous history of this spot (well told through park exhibits and guided tours of pictograph sites) are better reasons to visit Seminole Canyon State Park than mountain biking is, but since you're here, you might as well ride. The Rio Grande River Trail is a pleasant enough stroll across a rugged West Texas landscape from the park road to the point where Seminole Canyon opens up into the Rio Grande at the Amistad Reservoir.

Land status: State Historical Park, maintained by TPWD.

Maps: Free map at park headquarters; USGS Seminole Canyon.

Access: From Comstock, take U.S. 90 west 9 miles to the park entrance. Follow the park road past the headquarters to the parking area for the Rio Grande River Trail, on the left just before the camping area.

Notes on the trail: Though the ride here is not as spectacular as in some of the other state parks, the simple crossing of this land takes on an entirely new significance after browsing the historical exhibit at the park's interpretive center and taking a tour through the pictograph sites. The history of this canyon is conveyed in great detail in the exhibit—from the time the first *homo sapiens* wandered in 12,000 years ago through the passing of various hunter-gatherer tribes to expeditions by Spaniards and the U.S. Army to its acquisition by the parks department. It's an amazing story and will make your ride that much more enjoyable.

The ride itself is a fairly easy hour on the bike, though you'll likely extend that with a good sit-down by the Rio Grande. It's a right beautiful vista at the end of the trail, and from the final viewing point, you can just

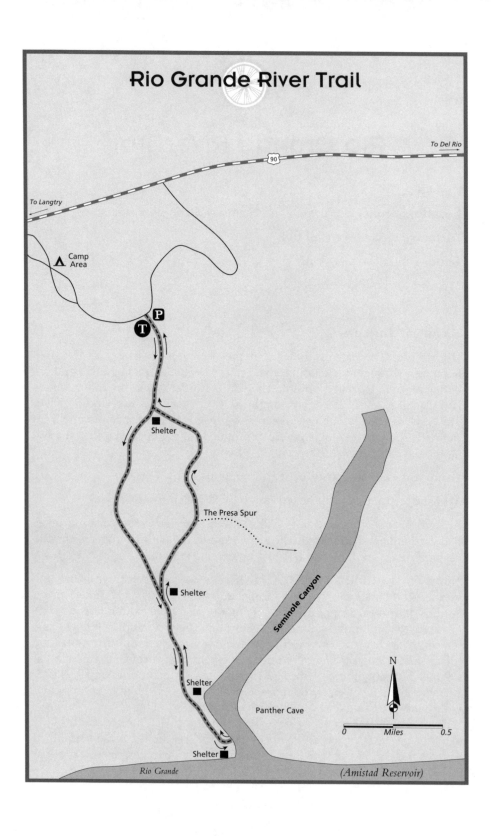

Rio Grande River Trail

90

To Del Rio

To Langtry

Camp Area

P

T

Shelter

The Presa Spur

Shelter

Seminole Canyon

Shelter

Panther Cave

N

0   Miles   0.5

Shelter

Rio Grande

(Amistad Reservoir)

A nice spot to stop: Seminole Canyon opening up into the Rio Grande.

barely see the Panther Cave rock-painting site on the other side of the canyon. Don't miss that one, either—sometimes they even do boat tours.

Before you set tire to trail, you'll see a pair of signs at the trailhead. One says STEEP CANYON DROP-OFFS, and the other says WATCH FOR SNAKES. Good advice, both. Though I didn't see any snakes or dive off any cliffs, a brutal wind blasted me with sand the whole time out. So watch for that at least.

The Ride

0.0   Ride out from the parking area past the signs on the clearly marked doubletrack. The terrain is flat and somewhat empty, save for an even spread of cactus and sand.

0.6   The center region of this trail is a big loop, and here's where you hit the front end of it. I went right, riding the other side on the return trip. I can't see as your direction would make any difference whatsoever. In fact, you might want to do a few laps on the loop before heading down to the river.

0.8 Off to the left side of the trail, a shelter with a slatted wooden roof and two benches is a very nice spot for a rest.

1.4 Here you'll reach the intersection at the far side of the loop. Continue south to get to the river. Just past the junction there's another wooden shelter and a sign that says SCENIC OVERLOOK 1 MILE.

2.0 A jeep road branches off to the right here; follow the arrow pointing straight the way you were going. The other path leads off toward a different part of the canyon—a nice side trip for another great view and, if you're lucky, a look at the goats that graze the other side.

2.4 The first of the shelters near the canyon's end.

2.6 At trail's end there's another shelter, along with signage about Panther Cave across the way. Supposedly you can see the red panther figure some 15 feet long off to the right of the cave. Regardless, it's a gorgeous spot. Hang for a while, then turn around and head back.

3.7 Back at the southern trail junction, turn right for the other side of the loop.

3.9 The trail starts to climb on its way up and over the small plateau.

4.4 The trail called The Presa heads off and down to the right to the canyon. It's a pretty steep drop of just over 100 feet, but the view is worth the climb back out. This spur adds about 1.6 miles to the ride. When I rode out here an entire film crew was set up and filming a music video on a plateau in view from this spot. Three girls in bright clothes were singing in front of a full band, all of them faking along to a cheesy pop recording, with the glorious desert setting behind them. Quite a surreal moment. I never did find out what that song was, either.

6.0 After climbing back out from the canyon's edge, take a right at the main trail and another right at the northern junction.

6.6 Back at the parking area.

San Angelo State Park

Location: San Angelo.

Distance: 19+ miles.

Time: 2 hours, and then some.

Tread: Mostly singletrack, some doubletrack.

Aerobic level: Moderate to strenuous.

Technical difficulty: 3 to 4.

Highlights: The low vegetation out here makes for an endless horizon, and the singletrack goes as far as the eye can see. Though they could be marked a bit better, the vast network of loops offers epic opportunities that it would take far more than a single day to exhaust.

Land status: State Park.

Maps: Free map at park headquarters; USGS Twin Buttes.

Access: There are two entrances to the park. To enter on the north side, take U.S. 87 north from San Angelo to FM 2288, then south to the north shore entrance. To access the park by the south entrance, as I did, take U.S. 67 south from San Angelo to FM 2288. Take this route north to the park entrance. From the entrance, proceed past the fee booth to the parking area by the Chaparral Group Shelter. The trail heads out from there.

Notes on the trail: Welcome to Concho Country. A relatively new addition to the state parks catalog, having been leased by TPWD in 1995, San Angelo State Park is a largely undeveloped strip of gorgeous Concho Valley land on the edge of the O. C. Fisher Reservoir, right next to the city of San Angelo. The park sits on a four-corners of sorts, where the high plains and the hill country meet north to south and the landscapes of East Texas (green flatland) and West Texas (arid hills) converge. It's a wonderfully isolated spot where bison, longhorn, and mountain bikers can roam to their heart's content.

Don't let that DISTANCE listing up above fool you: There are far more than 19 miles of trail out here. The park's info says that there are more than 50 miles of multiuse trail altogether, and there very well may be, but somehow, after wandering abike for well over two hours—having a blast,

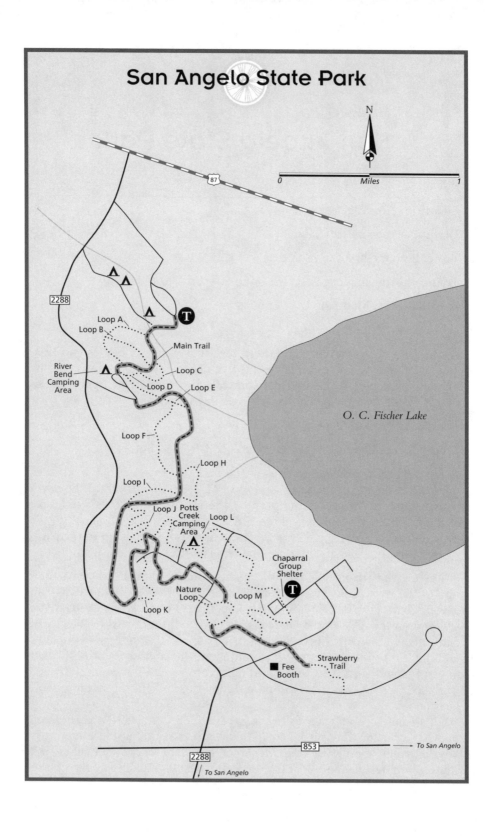

San Angelo State Park

87

N

0   Miles   1

2288

T

Loop A
Loop B
Main Trail
River
Bend
Camping
Area
Loop C
Loop D   Loop E

Loop F

Loop H

Loop I

Loop J Potts
Creek
Camping
Area
Loop L

Nature
Loop
Loop M

Loop K

O. C. Fischer Lake

Chaparral
Group
Shelter
T

Strawberry
Trail
Fee
Booth

853   → To San Angelo
2288
To San Angelo

I imagine this is quite a leafy canopy in the spring or summer. Here's brother Eric taking advantage of the fall temperatures at San Angelo State Park.

mind you, though never too sure of my bearings—I ended up where I began with just under 20 miles on the computer.

Time for a bit of honesty: I sorta got lost out here. The trails are amazing, and it looks simple enough on a map; but I was without compass, the day was totally overcast, and I was riding on a weekday, so there was no one around to ask for guidance. Excuses, excuses. The northern portion of the trail system is pretty well marked as loops break from the main trail and connect again down the line, but the southern half is a sprawling conglomerate of main paths and crisscrosses that can have the first-timer riding in circles. Even so, the riding—circular or otherwise—is loads of fun, ranging from steep, nasty stuff to long easy strolls. One piece of advice: Allow plenty of riding time.

The Ride

The main trail that stretches from one end of the park to the other is a long, relatively flat ride through the rolling hills of the Concho Valley. It's well marked and a challenge to your endurance and pedal-stroke, if not to your technical skills. From the concessions area near the Chaparral Group Shelter, the trail winds its way past the little Nature Trail loop, over the park road, and past the Potts Creek camping area. It's mostly solid dirt singletrack, clear of rocks and spiky plants, that will allow for some spinning of the big ring. Gradual climbs lead to easy descents, with the occasional drop thrown in to keep you honest.

The majority of the main trail is like this—pleasant and long and open. The loops that weave their way into and around the main trail offer a bit tougher riding, and once you get familiar enough with the lay of the land (as I did not), it seems you could piece together some pretty fantastic routes using the main trail as a connector from loop to loop. The loops are named—though not necessarily marked—from A to M, in order from north to south, and are only loops as such because they are cut at either end by the main trail. Confused? So was I. Suffice to say that if you think you're lost out here, you're not—whatever trail you're on eventually will spill back out onto the main trail, which is wide and well used.

The park's map helps a little bit, but don't depend on it (or the one in this book, either). A compass would be helpful, just to keep your bearings in a more general sense. As for the specifics, don't sweat them too much. Just ride until you can't ride anymore, then look for that main trail and head to whichever end of the park you left your vehicle. Vague, yes. But, hey, that's part of the fun, right?

X Bar Ranch

Location: Eldorado.

Distance: 12-mile loop.

Time: 2 hours.

Tread: Mostly singletrack, some doubletrack.

Aerobic level: Moderate to strenuous.

Technical difficulty: 3 to 4.

Highlights: A fine entry in the growing list of private ranches giving mountain bikers a go at their acreage, X Bar Ranch is one of the jewels of West Texas riding. It's quickly accessible to folks from most of Central

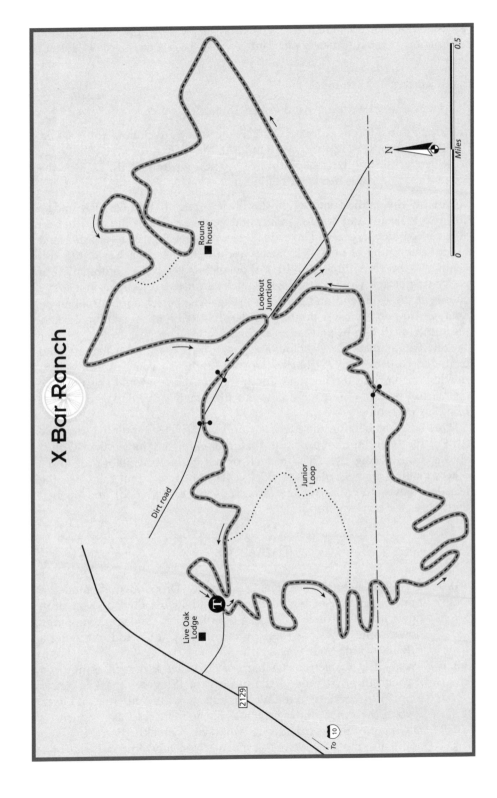

X Bar Ranch

Round house

Lookout
Junction

Dirt road

Junior
Loop

Live Oak
Lodge

T

2129

10

To

N

0   Miles   0.5

Texas' major metropolitan areas, which makes it a very appealing weekend destination. That it's such a pleasant place to pass a couple days doesn't hurt, either.

Land status: Private ranch land.

Maps: Free map with registration; USGS Eldorado SW.

Access: From Eldorado, take U.S. 277 south toward Sonora for 3 miles. Turn right onto FM 2129 and go 18 miles to the turn in for Live Oak Lodge (*past* the turnoff by the rock with X BAR RANCH written on it). Park by the lodge; the trail heads out from behind it.

Notes on the trail: Standing on the back porch of the Live Oak Lodge, you can look out and see for miles, and you'll rejoice at the fact that all you survey, you are about to ride. It's a gorgeous spread—a green and bristly conjoining of near West Texas and the farthest reaches of the Hill Country—and the riding is nothing short of fantastic. The combination of rocky singletrack winding through thick mesquite and juniper on a curvy course at the front end and long, sweeping stretches of doubletrack in an open pasture on the back half offers riders a little bit of everything, including some tough climbs and tricky descents.

The trail is marked red, blue, and green for expert, intermediate, and beginner, respectively. All flags are on the right, so you can easily keep moving in the right direction. A junior loop at the front end shortens the course to just a few miles and cuts out the tough stuff. So there's something for everyone.

This land has been in the Meador family for five generations, since the turn of the twentieth century, and the great care they have taken with it shows. Considering the dreadful lack of public land available for Texas bikers looking for new places to ride, we're very lucky that folks like the Meadors have cut trail systems (especially ones this good) and opened their acres for our exploration.

The Ride

0.0 Trailhead behind the Live Oak Lodge. Drop down behind the building and head out to the right. Right off the bat, you drop down a nasty little ledge, take a tight left turn, and work your way down some limestone steps. From there you'll wind out along a ridge, working your way south.

1.0 Twisty, flat singletrack of hard-packed dirt and rock brings you through the first mile to the turnoff for the green-marked junior loop. Turn left here to follow it; it cuts along the pipeline and back toward the ranch, hitting the end of the main trail as it returns.

1.2 Staying on the described ride, you'll hit a creekbed crossing, and you'll also cross a pipeline—I mean, physically, you and your bike cross over the pipeline. From there you climb out a steep, short hill and take a left. The trail flattens out again for a while before making you climb some more. You're going up and down along a ridge for a while.

1.7 The riding is fairly technical here, including some tight sloping turns and a few switchbacks.

2.1 Cross an open throughway. The trail turns to a fast, gradual descent.

2.4 A strip of whoop-de-dos that get you moving faster and faster sling you around trees and over rocks at a fast, smooth clip.

2.7 Cross a dirt road.

3.3 Pass through a gate—if it was closed in front of you, close it behind you. The trail leads off to the left, very clearly marked and getting faster all the time.

3.7 Now climb and drop in short, successive bursts, hitting a series of hills separated by fast, twisty singletrack.

4.3 Pass the water tanks, which you could see from the back porch of the lodge.

4.6 Lookout Junction. Take a right to complete the whole 12-mile loop, or take a left to cut it to 8 miles. You'll hit this junction again on the way back in from the 12-miler.

4.8 Shortly after turning right at Lookout Junction, you're on a screaming descent—a long, straight, open strip of doubletrack that'll render your big-ring-small-cog combination not big enough. Beware: There's a sharp left turn at the bottom, at exactly 5.0 miles.

6.1 A long climb in the wide open brings you up through the pasture on some exposed doubletrack.

6.4 A red arrow marking a left turn here is a bit hard to see because of a rock in the way—though that may have been changed by the time you read this. This signals the beginning of a strip of single-track that gets you out of the pasture for a mile or so.

7.0 A fairly long and gradual switchback brings you up just a bit before you cross a dirt road and get back onto the wide pasture trail.

8.2 Cross the road again.

8.5 Back at the trail junction connecting the front and back halves of the trail. Turn right.

8.8 Some more doubletrack brings you to a gate (close it behind you) and down a series of hills to the main road, where you'll go left and through another gate. An immediate left off the main road gets you back into the trees and onto the singletrack.

9.6 Climb some fairly steep, rocky stuff.

10.0 The Junior Loop rejoins the trail from the left.

10.9 Take a left turn off the ridge and head back down all the stuff you just climbed, back away from the trailhead, and down a set of switchbacks.

11.5   Come up off a steep climb and the lodge is in sight. This single-track brings you back in the opposite way you went out for a true loop.

11.7   Back at the lodge.

West Texas Honorable Mentions

(A) Lajitas Loop

Location: Lajitas.

Distance: 14-mile loop.

Time: 2 hours.

Tread: Mix of singletrack, doubletrack, and improved jeep road.

Aerobic level: Moderate to strenuous.

Technical difficulty: 3.

Highlights: That amazing Big Bend scenery is definitely the star attraction of this ride—though the trail itself is no slouch, either. A mix of dirt road, jeep road, and singletrack that winds its way across the rugged landscape of the outskirts of Lajitas, this trail is a must for any fan of West Texas terrain. It's also a prime spring destination for mountain-bike racers nation- and worldwide.

Land status: Some public land, some private, so obey all signs and adjust your route accordingly.

Maps: USGS Lajitas and Amarilla Mountain.

Access: If you want to pass through Big Bend National Park to get here, which usually requires paying the park fee, take U.S. 385 south from Marathon into the park to Panther Junction. Turn right at Panther Junction and follow TX 118 west past the Maverick entrance station and out of the park toward Study Butte. At Texas Highway 170 turn left and follow this route about 40 miles to Lajitas. Lajitas is on the far western edge of the National Park, but you have to leave the park in order to get to it, as the Mesa de Anguila area is not passable by road. If you want to bypass the park, head south from Alpine on TX 118 and turn left on TX 170. When you get to Lajitas, TX 170 goes right through the center of town. At the town square (very obvious), park in any of the available lots. The trail sets out at the bottom of the hill, just under the square. Head out along the road next to the airfield.

Notes on the trail: You'll probably want to check on the status of the route before you take off riding, as it changes fairly often. Desert Sports,

Brother John on high ground in Lajitas.

a guide/bike shop in Terlingua just east of the ghost town, is a good source of information on these trails. The town of Lajitas was auctioned off to an Austinite in spring 2000, and last I heard plans were in full swing to turn the town into a golf community. No kidding. Alas, the days of the scattered desert rat inhabitants with a beer-drinking goat for a mayor are gone for good, it seems. Perhaps the new crowd won't be able to stand the heat—literally.

The ride: This ride follows the race course, marked as it's been for the past few years of the Desert Challenge, the annual February NORBA race. It crosses a mix of wide-open public space and private ranchland that's graciously opened to bikes for the race and for most of the rest of the year, according to the locals. But, as the locals seem to be changing a bit, make sure it's still OK to ride out here before doing so. Obey signs and fences, as ranchers are known to protect what's theirs by some pretty severe means. Know what I mean?

The surface ranges from hard, rocky doubletrack to loose, sandy doubletrack, as well as hardpack and way-loose singletrack. Lots of sand in spots can pose a hazard to your balance, and you spend a good amount of time in the wide bed of Comanche Creek.

There are many more miles of riding out here than what you'll see in a day. The race course extends from the 14-mile beginner's loop to a 31-mile intermediate or sport loop and a 40-mile expert course—and that doesn't even cover all of it. Most of the outer portions are on ranch roads and may well be closed to the public when there's no race happening; again, check *before* heading out. There are some killer hills and some breathtaking vistas out in the far reaches, and you've come all the way out here, so you might as well ride as long as you can, right? If you manage to find a local to follow around, you'll be much better off; they most definitely know these trails and roads better than anyone else. As always, and more pressing than usual, take plenty of water and something to eat. Although the technical challenges aren't so severe, there's lots of miles to cover and lots of ways to get a flat or wander offtrack. Good luck—and have fun!

B El Solitario Road

Location: Big Bend Ranch State Park.

Distance: 16 miles, with options for much more or less.

Time: 2 hours, at least.

Tread: Unimproved jeep road and doubletrack.

Aerobic level: Moderate.

Technical difficulty: 3.

Highlights: Scenic views and solitude, especially the latter, can be found here like nowhere else in Texas. It seems that the views go on forever, and if you only had the time and the legs, so could you and your bike. Give it a shot.

Land status: State Park.

Maps: Free park map for basic layout; USGS El Solitario and Tascotal Mesa.

Access: From Presidio, take FM 170 east to Casa Piedra Road and turn left. Follow this road for 7 miles, then turn right on the main park road. After 2.4 miles, there is a gate—you must get the combination from park headquarters before setting out. It's about 25 miles from the gate to the Pila Montoya campsite, where you will park your vehicle and start the journey to El Solitario.

Notes on the trail: The first thing to remember when riding the unimproved roads of Big Bend Ranch is that this was, until recently, a working ranch. The roads here are laid out for the utilitarian purpose of crossing the park's acreage, not for scenic mountain bike loops. So while the serious off-roader with loads of time and energy to kill may be able to string together loops with some interesting cross-country trekking between main roads, most rides out here will be of the out-and-back variety. Side roads offer abundant opportunities for exploration and more and more miles; the scenery along the main jeep roads is stunning, too.

The ride: My riding partner and I first took off on the road heading through the campsite and south. This was the wrong way. It starts off with a nice, fast downhill that quickly turns into deep gravel dotted with formidable boulders. Not particularly fun riding, but it is a somewhat cleared path. After about 2 miles you'll cross a creekbed; at about 2.5 you'll come to a gate. Soon after that, the road peters out again.

For our second start, we went past the water tank and trough, through the gate and over a cattleguard, heading out on the road pointing eastward. A half mile in, a road breaks off to the left. At about 1 mile, there's a Y-shaped intersection. Heading left, it's long, sweeping downhills and climbs, over ridge after ridge, each revealing desert scenery that'll have you gaping as you're gasping. The surface alternates between hardpack and loose gravel, all of it doable, but taking a toll on the legs. After 3.4 miles, a road leads off to the right—hard-surfaced doubletrack that crosses creekbeds and heads over a ridge past a water tank, just one of many exploration options. At about 4.5 miles in this direction, you come to a residence—that's where we turned around.

There's lots to see out at this end of the park, and the best way to approach it is with plenty of time, water, and patience. The rewards—the views—are worth the trip.

Central Texas

Now we get to the heart of the state. This is where it all comes together—where the mountains of the West smooth out and the plains of the North and the Panhandle rise up into the scenic Hill Country; where the rolling piney woods of the East give way to cedar groves and the sandy southeastern terrain rises away from the Gulf of Mexico into the rocky hills of the Balcones Escarpment. This is not mountains, but this is prime mountain biking country nonetheless.

These are my stomping grounds, which is part of the reason the highest concentration of rides in the book is found here. Another reason is that there are more rides to do here. Private ranches and state parks throughout the Hill Country offer some of the most fun and challenging rides in Texas. What we lose to mountain states in elevation, we more than make up for in technical challenges. Boulders and roots, rock ledges to hop up and drop off, steep sections that'll bring you to a standstill on a climb and have your butt burned by your back tire on the descent—these are the characteristics of Hill Country riding, of places like Kelly Creek Ranch, the Hill Country State Natural Area, and Flat Rock Ranch. Easier rides like the Wolf Mountain Trail, Kerrville-Schreiner State Park, and the Upper Gorman Creek trail let you visit and experience the beauty of the Hill Country without subjecting yourself to its more tortuous aspects. Good rides all, and great places to spend a weekend.

In the midst of the middle, the center of it all, is the capital city—Austin. Outstanding restaurants, a wealth of parks and green spaces in and near downtown, and the most vibrant and ubiquitous music scene that I've ever been lucky enough to experience are some of the big draws of this strange hybrid of small town and big city. But, we're talking about biking, right?

While there are good rides to do in every region of the state, it's my humble opinion that we in Austin have it the best. For starters, we have the Barton Creek Greenbelt. At first glance (or ride), it seems innocuous enough—a long, flat snake of singletrack working its way along Barton Creek from the springs to the Hill of Life, seemingly the only climbing to do out here. But follow a local or explore the side trails on your own, and a whole 'nother world of big hills and seldom-traveled singletrack opens up to you. And if the Greenbelt is the yin, then the Emma Long Motocross Park (or City Park, as the locals call it), is most definitely the yang. There will be many who disagree, but to my mind, body and bike, this is the most difficult and abusive—and the most fun—ride going. Steep climbs lead to big limestone shelves to drop off to more and more of the same. I don't think I've ever really been "freeriding" (whatever that means), but this is what I think of when I hear of people hucking big drops and beating themselves up on crazy trails. Be careful here. Ride *only* if you're experienced and have good control of your rig.

While these two are the most popular rides, there are plenty more right in town (Walnut Creek, the Homestead Trail) and just outside town (Muleshoe, Rocky Hill Ranch) that cover all levels of riding. One of the longstanding rides just east of town, Bluff Creek Ranch in Warda, is up for sale at the time of this writing. It's not yet clear whether the new owners will continue the bike-friendly use of the land here, but one thing's for sure: Doc Nolan, former proprietor of Bluff Creek, has done as much for mountain biking in this state as just about anyone, and his presence—not to mention his trails—will be sorely missed. And though they've also suffered some heavy losses trailwise, San Antonio still has some good riding in McAllister Park, as well as the promise of a whole new system in the soon-to-open Government Canyon State Park. The addition of Flat Rock Ranch in Comfort, an easy drive from San Antonio, has been a blessing to the mountain bike community there.

Many, many trails, most of them with nearby camping facilities, make Central Texas a fantastic place to live and a prime destination for a long weekend visit. This is the place to develop the skills that will make mountain biking elsewhere easier and more enjoyable. Balance, power, agility, and speed: These are the things to bring with you—and, of course, your bike. See you soon.

Hermit's Trace/Cougar Canyon

Location: Hill Country State Natural Area, Bandera.

Distance: 9-mile loop.

Time: 1.5 hours.

Tread: Mix of singletrack and doubletrack.

Aerobic level: Moderate.

Technical difficulty: 3.

Highlights: This setting is as pure Texas Hill Country as you're gonna find. Sharp inclines and thorny vegetation abound on the many miles of trail in this state park, offering more space for exploration than you can likely cover in any given weekend. The trails, numerous and mazelike as they are, are very well marked and fairly well maintained.

Land status: State Natural Area, maintained by TPWD.

Maps: Free map at park headquarters; USGS Tarpley Pass.

Access: From Bandera, take Texas Highway 173 south across the Medina River. Turn right at Texas Highway 1077 and follow this for about 10 miles to the end of the pavement, then continue on the gravel road to the park entrance. Turn right past park headquarters and continue past the Bar-O camping area to the parking lot on the left. This trail takes off from just past the parking area on your right.

Notes on the trail: Horses and the folks who ride them are the main users of the trails in the Hill Country SNA, so be on your guard—and be courteous when you approach them. Etiquette says that you stop your progress and stick to the low side of the trail, letting horses pass, and speaking in a low voice so as not to spook them. Being thrown by a horse is nasty business, so do all you can to keep horses calm—and the trails open to mountain bikes.

Aside from all that, feel free to ride until you can't ride anymore. There are many, many miles of trail out here, which I've attempted to break up into a few different loops. Following the routes I've described here requires some pretty specific sets of turns, which may be a bit too stringent for some of you independent types. That's fine—just hit the trail and

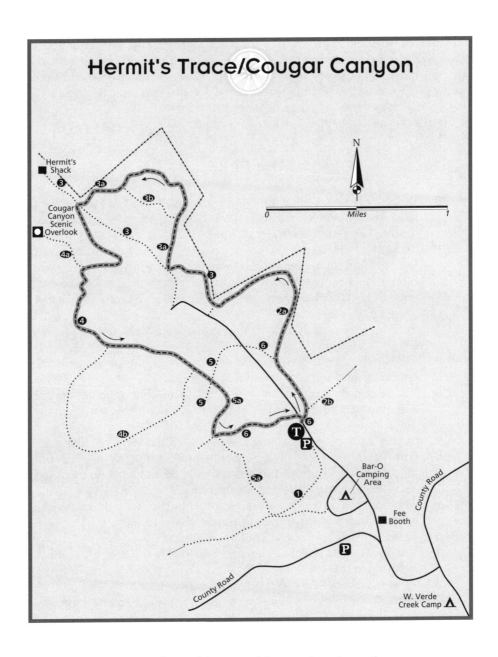

Hermit's Trace/Cougar Canyon

go. You should bring the park's map with you, though, as there are no THIS WAY TO YOUR CAR signs and you can get pretty far away from where you began with little effort.

There are some steep, nasty sections out here, too, so be careful and keep your eyes out on the trail ahead of you. It's all very rocky terrain, with plenty of opportunities for spectacular endos if you're not paying attention—and with scenery this captivating, it's easy to space out.

One last warning: Much of the area covered by trail out here is not covered by trees, which means that big Texas sun will likely be beating down on you most of the time you're riding. Be aware of its effects, and take along plenty of water. Nothing ruins a ride for you and your partners like collapsing from dehydration or heat stroke.

That said, have a ball!

The Ride

0.0   Parking area near the equestrian camp area. Head out to the park road and go left for a hundred yards or so, then turn right onto Trail 6. Continue past the sign for Trail 2b.

0.5   Trail 2a. This takes you down an easy grade to the fenceline, which you'll follow for a while, keeping it on your right. There are more than a couple creek crossings along the way, and I was lucky enough to ride when there was actually water in them. This is not always the case.

1.3   Turn right at Trail 3, away from the road, staying along the fenceline.

1.6   Take another right onto Trail 3a, heading back out toward the park boundary and the sizable hill just ahead.

2.4   The trail passes up and over that hill, providing a bit of a grunt going up and your first taste of these rocky descents on your way down.

2.9   Skinny little bit of singletrack leads off to the left from the wide path you're on—that's where you wanna be. It's not marked, but take it anyway. It drops through a creekbed and hops up the other side, sending you out along a ridgeline.

3.6   Another fun little drop brings you all the way down to the creekbed on a steep grade with some sharp turns.

3.8   Pass the other end of the Trail 3b cut-across.

4.1   Where Trail 3a meets 3, go right to reach the Hermit's Shack camping area.

4.3   Hermit's Shack. Turn around and head back.

4.7   Butterfly Springs campsite on the right is easy to miss on the way out.

5.1   Cross the creek at this junction, and take a right onto Trail 4.

5.4   Trail 4a leads off to the right to a scenic vista of Cougar Canyon. It's well worth the trip. You get some good singletrack here, tracing ridgelines and charging through a couple nice meadows.

5.9   Downhill bomb—watch your speed. There's a turnoff to the Trail 4b loop, the entrance to which was barred by brush when I rode— a polite way to say "keep your butt off this trail." Other sections were blocked off, too, in an attempt to save delicate areas from damage. Respect these barriers.

6.8 Passing Boyle's House on the left, continuing on Trail 4.

7.2 A right turn onto Trail 5 takes you out toward the Twin Peaks area of the park. This, too, was closed when I rode here, but if it's open when you pass by, take it. Instead, I veered left on Trail 6, cutting this ride a bit short.

7.8 Connect with the road and turn right, passing Trail 2, a piece of doubletrack that runs parallel to the road.

8.0 Back at the parking area.

Wilderness Trail/Bandera Creek

Location: Hill Country State Natural Area, Bandera.

Distance: 7-mile loop.

Time: 1 hour.

Tread: Mix of doubletrack and singletrack.

Aerobic level: Moderate.

Technical difficulty: 4.

Highlights: This loop offers a great blend of steady flatland riding and a nice climb up (and descent down) Ice Cream Hill in the far west corner of the park. The route back from the hill follows Bandera Creek, crossing and recrossing it in some tight and swervy singletrack.

Land status: State Natural Area, maintained by TPWD.

Maps: Free map at park headquarters; USGS Tarpley Pass.

Access: From Bandera, take TX 173 south across the Medina River. Turn right at TX 1077 and follow this for about 10 miles to the end of the pavement, then continue on the gravel road to the park entrance. Turn right past park headquarters and continue past the Bar-O camping area to the parking lot on the left. Trail 1 takes off from the part of the parking area toward headquarters.

Notes on the trail: Though the front end of the trail might lull you into blissful spaciness, keep your wits about you for the trip up and over Ice Cream Hill. As with most riding out here, the going's not terribly difficult,

Wilderness Trail/Bandera Creek

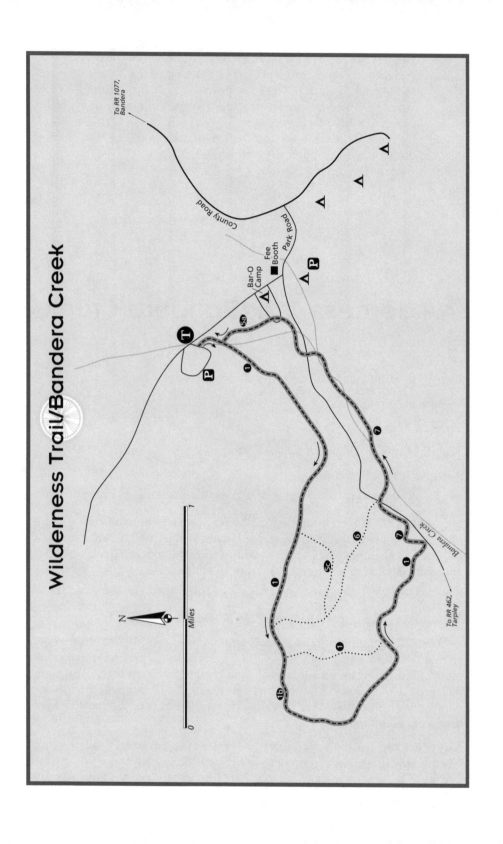

Greener days at the Hill Country State Natural Area. It's not always so lush, but it's always good riding.

but it's pretty easy to tumble if you're not paying attention. The return trip along and through Bandera Creek is soggy after rain and speedy after drought, so plan accordingly.

Keep in mind that they don't call this the Cowboy Capital for nothing. Lots of folks ride horses out here, and they don't take kindly to spandex-clad speed demons spooking their mounts and spoiling their outings. Be on the lookout for equestrians, and be courteous when you see them. Yield the trail, give 'em a polite howdy, and let them pass before continuing on your ride. That way we bikers will get to keep riding here.

The Ride

0.0 Parking area near the equestrian camp area. Facing the road, head out to your right on Trail 1. Lots of little trails crisscross the main path here, but just keep on going. There's a little bit of a hill to get the blood pumping, too.

0.8 Junction of Trail 5a; stay on Trail 1.

1.3 Junction of Trail 1a, taking off to the left to meet the road. Pass this, too, staying on Trail 1. The trail is doubletrack here, completely unprotected, with a fairly rough surface due to hoofprints. Get used to it; they're everywhere.

1.4 Cross Trail 6.

1.8 At this intersection Trail 5 goes to the right and Trail 5c goes to the left, right up that nasty-looking hill. Stay on Trail 1.

2.5 Here's where you break off. Trail 1b takes off to the right for the trip over Ice Cream Hill. Staying on Trail 1 will take you to a pond and a great spot for a break. But you don't want a break, do you? Hit Trail 1b and get climbing!

3.2 At the top of that long, rocky grunt, you'll have a spectacular view of your surroundings—the Hill Country at its very, very finest. Breathe deep, enjoy the vista, and steel yourself for the descent.

3.9 Hit the bottom running, weaving along the fenceline back toward Trail 1. When you hit it, take it to the right, keeping to the fenceline.

5.0 Near the road, pick up Trail 7 with a sharp cut back to the left. You don't actually reach the road. On Trail 7, hit a small gear for a quick, steep climb.

5.4 At the three-way intersection go right, down, and across the road. There should be some water to cross in Bandera Creek.

6.0 Another creek crossing.

6.7 Note the pond on the left right here as you zig and zag your way through the low-lying areas. I imagine this would be pretty fast if the terrain were dry, as it no doubt usually is.

7.2 Cross the road just down from headquarters.

7.7 After crossing the Bar-O camp area, you'll cover a bit more trail to reach the spot where you started.

Pasture Loop

Location: Hill Country State Natural Area, Bandera.

Distance: 6-mile loop.

Time: 45 minutes.

Tread: Mix of doubletrack and singletrack.

Aerobic level: Easy.

Technical difficulty: 2.

Highlights: An easy ride with manageable grades throughout, this is the place for beginners to test their wheels before tackling the other trails listed here. A simple loop with two small extension loops wanders through the eastern corner of the park, offering serene meadow views and a couple small hills to get you up and looking around.

Land status: State Natural Area, maintained by TPWD.

Maps: Free map at park headquarters; USGS Tarpley Pass.

Access: From Bandera, take TX 173 south across the Medina River. Turn right at TX 1077 and follow this for about 10 miles to the end of the pavement, then continue on the gravel road to the park entrance. At the intersection stay to the left, away from the residence and headquarters (provided you've paid your fees, of course), and continue to the parking lot across from the Chaquita Falls camping area. The trail begins across the road, heading out to the east on Trail 9.

Notes on the trail: This ride is about as peaceful as they come, a quiet saunter through stands of oak and cedar lined with plenty of grasses and cacti. This is a trail that anyone can handle, so bring your kids or novice friends or significant others and introduce them to the joys of two-wheel travel. It's a nice mix of singletrack and doubletrack that sees mostly horse traffic—so the surface will be somewhat less than pristine. In fact, in some spots it's downright rutted with hoofpits, but that's the breaks.

Until recently, bikers were considered something of a nuisance here, and our access to the trails was limited. But on my last visit, they'd decided to test the waters—no doubt to increase visitation—and had made all the trails here all-access. They hadn't removed all the NO BIKE signs,

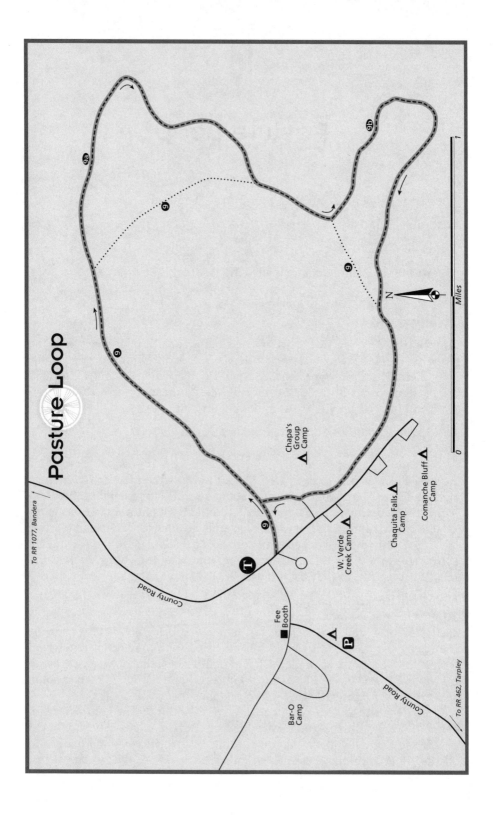

Pasture Loop

To RR 1077, Bandera

County Road

County Road

To RR 462, Tarpley

Fee Booth

Bar-O Camp

W. Verde Creek Camp

Chapa's Group Camp

Chaquita Falls Camp

Comanche Bluff Camp

N

Miles

0

though, and there were a few along this trail. But it's legal to ride, so mount up and explore away.

With so many horses about, bikers need to mind our manners out here. Those big critters can be easily spooked, and nasty things happen when they react badly to an approaching biker (which leads to even nastier reactions from the riders and park personnel). Keep to the low side of the trail, if there is one. If there isn't, just step off the path, give a friendly how-do, and talk low as the equestrians make their way past. Once clear, proceed. And thank you—you've just scored some positive points for our side in the ongoing biker-equestrian battle.

The Ride

0.0 Parking area across from Chaquita Falls. Cross the street and head out on Trail 9. This description traces the route clockwise. The surface is doubletrack, nice and flat.

0.3 A gentle climb gets you up a bit for a better view of the surrounding land. In spring loads of tiny purple flowers dot the ground, and thistles grow to about 4 feet high, adorned with gigantic purple flowers themselves. The dry, golden grass waves in the breeze, making this a scene right out of a movie.

0.8 Trail 2b breaks off to the left here, which can be followed to the west to hook up with the Bar-O Pasture Trail and then to any other trail in the park. Stay to the right for now.

1.2 The turnoff for Trail 9b goes to the left. There are two turnoffs, and it doesn't matter which you take. Just remember that if you take the first one, stay to the left at the intersection that closely follows it; otherwise you'll get back on Trail 9 and unintentionally skip the loop. Trail 9b bends to the right and follows the fenceline up a gentle hill, changing from hoof-pocked singletrack to nice doubletrack, and back down to meet Trail 9.

2.9 Shortly after reconnecting with the main Trail 9, there's another turnoff to the left for 9b. This loop's all but completely flat, a very pretty ride out and back for about a mile and a half.

4.5 The Trail 9b loop meets Trail 9 again; turn left, recrossing the fenceline and following Trail 9c along the road. This is doubletrack, somewhat shaky with hoofmarks. If it's real bad, or wet, you can jump off the trail and use the road here.

5.5 Chapa's group camping area is on your right here.

6.0 Back where you started, turn left to return to the road and the parking area.

Hightower Loop

Location: Hill Country State Natural Area, Bandera.

Distance: 6-mile loop.

Time: 1 to 1.5 hours.

Tread: Mostly doubletrack, some singletrack.

Aerobic level: Moderate.

Technical difficulty: 3.

Highlights: This is one of the somewhat challenging rides in the park, as the trail traverses a couple decent hills and allows plenty of spots to get your speed up. It's not horribly difficult, but it does pose a few tests of the vertical sort. I'd have to say that the best parts of this ride are the swimming holes along West Verde Creek, which runs parallel to the road. Make sure you come prepared for the chance to cool down in one of them.

Land status: State Natural Area, maintained by TPWD.

Maps: Free map at park headquarters; USGS Tarpley Pass.

Access: From Bandera, take Texas Highway 173 south across the Medina River. Turn right at Texas Highway 1077 and follow this for about 10 miles to the end of the pavement, then continue on the gravel road to the park entrance. Proceed to headquarters, take care of any fees you need to pay (for day use or camping, depending on your plans), and park by the Bar-O camping area. Trail 8 leads out from just across the street from headquarters, heading roughly south.

Notes on the trail: The Hightower Loop is a combination of Trails 8, 8a, and 8b, which skirt the southern edge of the park, going out and around the West Verde Creek, Chaquita Falls, and Comanche Bluff camp areas. Obviously, one of these places would be a good camping spot if you were spending a couple days out here, which I heartily recommend.

As with any trail here, there's a good chance you'll come across some horse and/or hiker traffic. Be courteous and yield the trail. We have the mechanical advantage over folks afoot, and our steel steeds don't freak out quite as easily as a horse does. Let them pass with a friendly howdy (this is cowboy land, after all), and continue on your way when the coast is

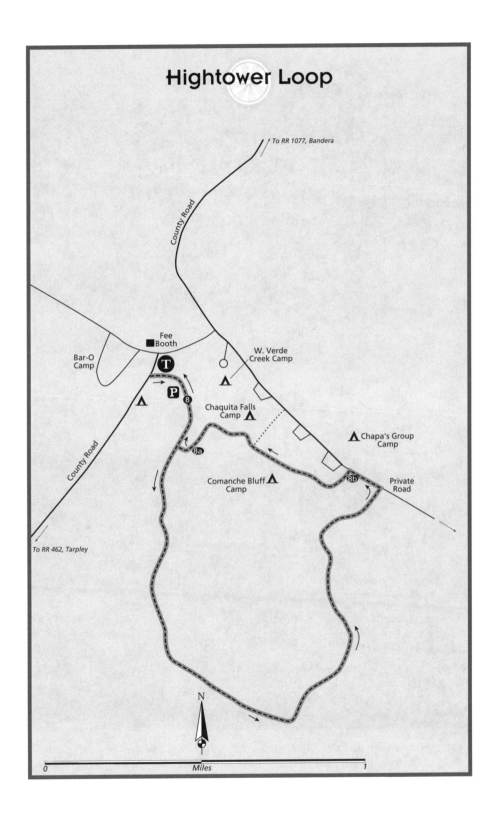

Hightower Loop

To RR 1077, Bandera

County Road

Fee
Booth

Bar-O
Camp

W. Verde
Creek Camp

T

P 8

Chaquita Falls
Camp

8a

Chapa's Group
Camp

County Road

Comanche Bluff
Camp

8b

Private
Road

To RR 462, Tarpley

N

0   Miles   1

The drops are steep and plentiful along the Hightower Loop. Be sure to watch for our six-legged friends—equestrians, that is. They're everywhere out here, and it's not always easy to hear them coming over the clatter of your rig.

clear. Everyone's happiest when bikers are polite, and it seems that we two-wheel enthusiasts have been allowed into the Hill Country SNA on a trial basis. Let's not lose access to these trails.

On that same note: On more than a few parts of this loop, you'll be tempted to let loose and bomb down some of these hills like you're on an Olympic slalom course. Don't give in. Maintain control, at whatever speed that is a possibility for you, and keep your head up. Bike versus horse equals a nasty collision you don't want any part of.

Another thing to consider: Bandera is home to some mighty fine nightlife. If you do spend a couple nights here, leave the park for a cold Lone Star with the friendly locals at one of the downtown watering holes. It's a great cap to a great day out here, worth skipping a few hours of campfire time.

The Ride

This trail was not open on my last visit. It was wet then, though, and a few spots were taped off and restricted from use. However, I had ridden this loop a few times previously, and last I heard it had been reopened. As always, heed trail closings and choose your rides accordingly.

You can begin this ride from either the beginning of Trail 8, right across the road from park headquarters, or on a spur to Trail 8a that heads out from the parking area between the West Verde Creek and Chaquita Falls camp areas. Starting near the headquarters, Trail 8 leads out on double-track for about a third of a mile before passing the junction for Trail 8a. I rode counterclockwise, keeping to the right at this intersection and following the doubletrack. It's a good surface, carrying you over a few gradual ridges and up a couple short, steep climbs.

At about the 2-mile mark, after crossing a couple fencelines at their meeting, the trail takes a left turn and heads up a pretty serious climb. This is where you slide that butt forward to the point of the seat, get in as small a gear as you need, shift your weight forward, and hammer your way up. It's rocky and parts of it are loose, but you can do it. Keep your rhythm and get to the top. Up there it flattens out briefly before bending left and plunging down the other side of the hill you just climbed. Watch it, because this is as loose as the other side, and there are a few ledges to be aware of. Move your butt back and let the bike do the work—and be careful.

After this drop, the trail planes out a bit again, still doubletrack, and crosses another fenceline, curving around to the east in speedy fashion. Again, the surface is good, perhaps solid enough to be impervious to hoofs.

Just shy of the 5-mile mark, a junction has Trail 8b heading off to the left. Take a left, crossing the creek again and heading up toward Trail 8a, which runs parallel to the road. There are some nice, quick sections in here, and you have the option of crossing the road and doing Trail 9 as well. I'd stay on Trail 8a all the way back up to 8. Trail 9 is another ride altogether.

Trail 8a gives you some singletrack to contend with—a speedy mile or so that shoots along West Verde Creek through cedar groves and past tons of cacti, so watch your ankles. This is where those swimming holes are—one of them right by the Comanche Bluff camp area and the other, better, one just below the Chaquita Falls camp area. Take a break; you've earned it. When you hit Trail 8, turn right; and it's a short jaunt up this double-track back to the car.

Kelly Creek Ranch

Location: Near Hunt.

Distance: 16 miles (two 8-mile loops).

Time: 2.5 hours.

Tread: Singletrack.

Aerobic level: Strenuous.

Technical difficulty: 5.

Highlights: Rocks. Lots of them. This trail is a test of will and fortitude, a challenge to get going when the going gets tough. It's also a well-laid course, with plenty of technical descents and tough climbs to keep the ride interesting.

Land status: Private ranch.

Maps: Free map available with registration; USGS Hunt.

Access: From U.S. 290 in Fredericksburg, take TX 16 south to Kerrville. Turn right onto TX 27 and head west to Ingram. In Ingram take TX 39 west toward Hunt. After the road crosses the Guadalupe River, stay to the left at the Y. The ranch is down this road about 2 miles on the right. The trailhead is in the field at the end of the parking area. This ride defines the North Loop first, followed by the South Loop.

Notes on the trail: When planning a trip out on the Kelly Creek trails, keep in mind that the going out here can be pretty slow, considering the

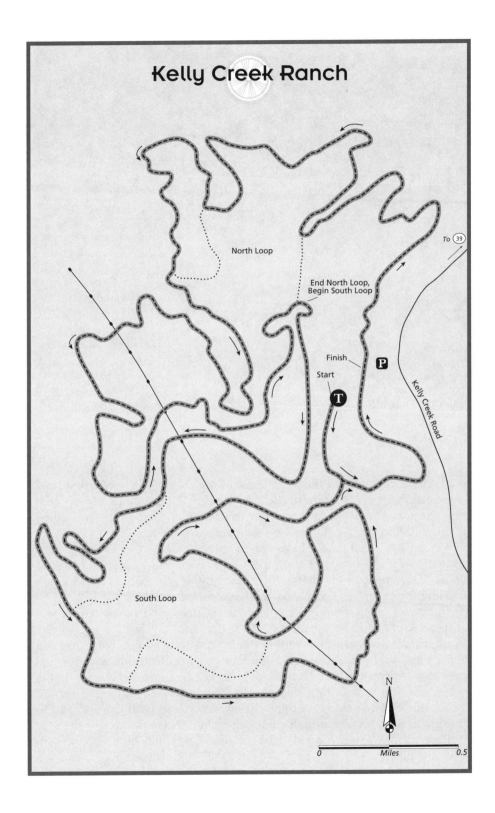

Kelly Creek Ranch

North Loop

End North Loop,
Begin South Loop

Finish

Start

South Loop

To 39

Kelly Creek Road

P

T

N

0   Miles   0.5

Looks dangerous, doesn't it? There are no casual, easy rides at Kelly Creek Ranch. Bring your climbing shoes.

often steep inclines and the abundance of big rocks. If it's your first time around these trails, be careful. Be very careful. There are plenty of spots that can toss you off your steed quicker than you can shout "endo," and plenty of blind drops that are best approached with caution.

The trails are marked for beginner and expert riders—the expert sections being rife with the steepest and most treacherous of the drops. I'd suggest doing the beginner route first, which has many tough spots of its own, and tackling the expert sections once you feel comfortable with the rest.

One other suggestion:67 Be sure your rig is in good repair before you grapple with the Kelly Creek trails. My first time hitting the expert sections, my rear wheel was a bit less than completely sound. A few broken spokes and many rock-banging attempts at wheel-truing later, I learned just how far you can stretch a set of V-brakes to accommodate a wobbly wheel and still be able to make the end of the trail.

For the 2001 fall race, the folks at Kelly Creek cut both loops in half to make a shorter, less daunting course. That's not to say that this is the way it'll be marked when you ride it. Your best bet would be to stop at Hill Country Bicycle Works in Kerrville on TX 27 just west of TX 16 and ask about the course. You can also pay your riding fees and get a map here.

The Ride

There are so many trails out here and so many ways to link them together into loops that it's fairly impossible to guess what route is going to be marked, if any, on any given visit. They hold NORBA-sanctioned races here at least once a year, and between the markers laid for the races and the maintenance efforts of the fine folks at Hill Country Bicycle Works, there usually is some sort of marked route.

According to the rough map they hand out when you register—whether at the ranch itself or at the bike shop prior to arrival—the preferred sequence is North Loop first, followed by the South Loop. However, on my last trip here the trails were routed the opposite way, and since then the trails have been altered entirely, shortening each loop into a faster, smoother version of itself. It seemed to work well, so chances are you'll ride two 4-mile loops when you visit the ranch—unless they've changed their mind again by then.

Whatever the marked route, there are two loops—each as strenuous and as treacherous as the other. The beginning of either loop can be found in the open pasture just west of (or behind) the parking area along the road in. Rolling into the start area, the North Loop heads out to the right and the South Loop to the left.

North Loop

The North Loop starts out bombing back and forth through a creekbed before sending you up Bowman Hill, close to 200 feet of elevation gain in about 0.5 mile. From there it's a series of steep drops and steep climbs, all studded with boulders from baby head to wagon wheel size. Sections of this trail carry the names Fat Man's Dilemma, Goat Ledge, and Devil's Switchback, which give a sense of the terrain to come. Red arrows usually mark the way, and the end of this loop will be the beginning of the next, and vice versa.

South Loop

The South Loop starts out of the same field as the North Loop but heading in the opposite direction. The South Loop is a bit rougher than the North; there are more long, rocky washes that are no fun and a lot of work. Even the downhills make you work on this half of the ranch, as the effort required to keep upright and on your bike obliterates any chance at using the descents to recover from the climbs. Just keep at it, be careful, and get through it. The good news is that it gets easier and more fun with familiarity, and the benefits that riding this trail will have on your technical skills and cardiovascular endurance are definitely worthwhile. What doesn't kill you makes you stronger. Now get out there and have a good time.

Kerrville-Schreiner State Park Trail

Location: Kerrville.

Distance: 4 miles.

Time: 30 minutes.

Tread: Mix of singletrack and doubletrack service roads.

Aerobic level: Easy.

Technical difficulty: 2.

Highlights: Classic, rugged Hill Country scenery and terrain in an easy-to-complete loop. A couple minimally difficult inclines offer the boulders and steep pitches of rougher Central Texas rides without the long miles and killer hills.

Land status: State Park.

Maps: Free park map; USGS Legion.

Access: From Kerrville, take Texas Highway 16 south to Texas Highway 173 and go west. Just after the junction with Loop 534, the park entrance appears on your right. The ride starts along the southern half of Park Road 19 at a small pullout between the group shelter and the Fox Run Loop.

Notes on the trail: Although Kerrville-Schreiner State Park is not a place I'd necessarily make the focus of a long mountain bike trip, it does have a nice little bike trail—just in case you find yourself in the area and don't want to risk life and limb over at Kelly Creek Ranch. This place packs enough campsites to rival any KOA, and the visitors tend to travel largely in RVs, so don't expect peaceful isolation if you're camping on a weekend. But the park is typically beautiful Hill Country scenery, and all the amenities are available.

Though the ride here is mostly an easy one, there are a couple of spots you won't want to snooze through. There's a pretty fun downhill just after the very first section, and there's a nice rocky wash you have to climb at about a mile and a half. At the farthest end of the loop, the trail marked orange has got some tight technical maneuvers that will check

Kerrville-Schreiner State Park Trail

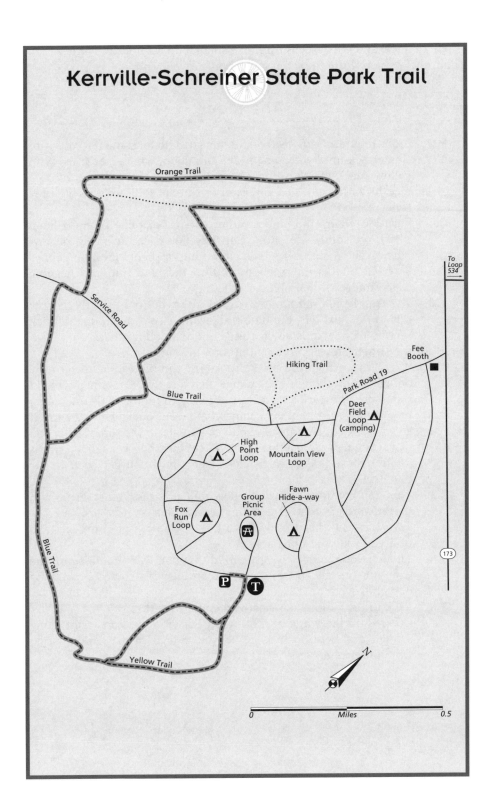

Orange Trail

Service Road

To Loop 534

Hiking Trail

Fee Booth

Blue Trail

Park Road 19

Deer Field Loop (camping)

High Point Loop

Mountain View Loop

Fox Run Loop

Group Picnic Area

Fawn Hide-a-way

Blue Trail

173

P T

Yellow Trail

N

0   Miles   0.5

your balance, and the descent from this small loop is quite fast. Other than that, there's very little to be nervous about.

The Ride

0.0 From the trailhead, head out about 0.1 mile on some flat, pleasant singletrack until you come to the first loop, which is marked with yellow markers. We went left here, starting the yellow trail on a nice little descent, and followed this about 0.25 mile to the blue trail.

0.4 Turn left where the blue trail begins—it looks like a runoff here. There are some side paths, but they don't lead to much of anywhere. The main trail winds out and up a slight elevation gain.

0.8 Stay left at this intersection, still on the blue trail and heading west. You're still climbing a little bit.

1.0 The trail bends right onto a service road, but only briefly. Follow this to the next left, the blue trail again, also a rough doubletrack service road. It dips down a little and then climbs back out, heading straight toward a big bump of a hill.

1.4 A left turn brings you up a clipped-off climb, heading toward the orange trail—though the orange markers were missing when I rode here, the park's map is pretty easy to follow. This trail starts up a rocky wash that gets somewhat steep, but it's over before it gets too tough. And just as soon as you get to the top, it spits you back down a somewhat rocky, technical descent that winds around rocks and through close trees until you get back to the blue trail.

2.1 The trail continues its slight downhill progress; long singletrack that rewards persistent pedaling with a nice, speedy stretch.

3.0 Turn right and head back down the service road toward the blue trail you rode out on.

3.5 Though you may not have realized that you were climbing on the way out, the return trip down the blue trail becomes a nice long downhill section.

3.8 Back to the yellow loop again; keep to the left to ride the half you skipped on the way out. The trail gets wide and runs right along a ridge, and before you know it, you're back at the parking area. One more time?

Flat Rock Ranch

Location: Comfort.

Distance: 2 loops, 9 miles each.

Time: 3 hours.

Tread: Mostly singletrack, very little jeep road.

Aerobic level: Strenuous.

Technical difficulty: 4.

Highlights: Long, long lines and wide open terrain will make you feel like you've got the entire Hill Country at your disposal. Flat Rock's 18+ miles of trail offer serious climbs and blazing descents in a gorgeous setting for a ride that captures the spirit of true cross-country.

Land status: Privately owned; fees required to ride and/or camp.

Maps: Map online at www.flatrockranch.com; USGS Comfort.

Access: Take U.S. 87 to Comfort. Just south of the intersection of I–10 and U.S. 87, turn left on FM 473. Proceed 1 mile to Flat Rock Road and turn left. Go through the gate, closing it behind you, and park near the first house on the left. The trailhead is on the main road near the house. From the parking area, head back out the way you came and turn in on the first path on the right.

Notes on the trail: This place puts the "Hill" in Hill Country. Long climbs that lead to long descents are in short supply on Texas trails, which makes Flat Rock Ranch a prime MTB destination for anyone looking to stretch out a bit.

There are some pretty good technical challenges out here, but they definitely play second fiddle to the overall scope of the ride, which comprises two sprawling loops totaling more than 18 miles that'll have you feeling like you've died and gone to singletrack heaven.

Ranch owner Jimmy Dreiss has gone all out to make this an appealing recreational destination and a viable race course and has succeeded admirably in both pursuits. San Antonio folks will be especially pleased, as this is close enough to their city limits for a day trip.

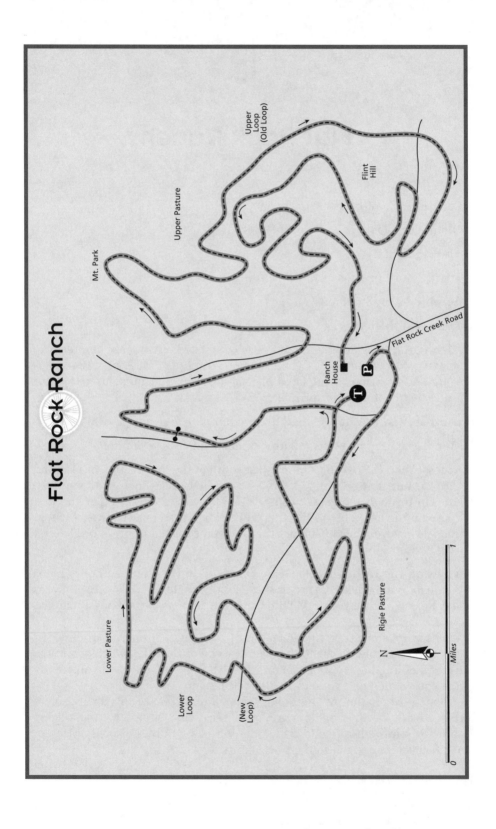

New Loop

0.0 The trail heads down to the creek, crosses, and brings you up into the hills on the other side.

0.6 After passing through a gate, the beginner's trail diverts to the right as the sport/expert trail heads left. It's well marked, so don't worry about losing the way. The advanced trail starts climbing shortly after this point, and though you get a few brief breaks, the climb continues for about 1.5 miles.

1.5 The trail passes through a gate and up a gentle grade, which then turns into a not-so-gentle grade. When it planes out, the trail goes off-camber; when it returns to level, it starts climbing again.

1.9 Here you clear the ridge into a wide meadow strewn with baby-head boulders; from there the trail takes a couple sharp, inclined turns before it begins to snake around and work its way down.

2.0 A long climb deserves a long downhill, and this one definitely qualifies. Gradual slopes provide long lines as the trail switchbacks down the side of this hill. That creek bottom is pretty far below you here, and though you may not be going all the way down, you'll get close.

2.5 Hit a high section of the creek, briefly, and then shoot back up on some embedded chain link on the other side. After winding through some quick ups and downs, the trail turns to another long, fast downhill.

3.5 After a bit of a climb you'll cross a dirt road and then head back down. The trail is again a bit off-camber, but not severely so. And the corners are *real* nice, so dive into those suckers.

4.1 Some switchbacks will get you up on a ridge that offers another spectacular Hill Country view. From here it's another long road down, but this one is punctuated by one of the ranch's steeper climbs—and it comes suddenly. Then the trail evens out for a bit before winding its way back up a long climb.

5.0 Though it seems like the lowlands here, this breezy meadow is a prelude for yet another long descent. You'll blaze for about 0.5 mile before taking a break to the right and shooting up another steep climb. The lower areas of the trail can be technically tricky, so keep your eyes out ahead of your wheel down there.

5.8 A couple of nice little boulder obstacles will signal the start of a long climb, steep switchbacks leading to an easier grade that takes you over the top of the dome-shaped hill.

7.1 Another gorgeous ridgetop where you can catch your breath and prepare for the descent—and this one's a bomb, too. Do not begrudge the climbing out here; the pay-offs are more than worth the effort. There are a couple more long climbs and seemingly longer descents over the next 2 miles.

9.0 The trail hits the doubletrack here, and just ahead there's a split that gives you the option of returning to the parking area to the right or heading left into the Old Loop.

Old Loop

0.0 Split in trail: FINISH ONLY to the right; Old Loop is to the left.

0.3 The trail crosses the creek again, climbs out, and heads through a gate. Don't forget to leave the gates as you found them.

1.6 After rolling up and over a couple short, hard-packed hills, you'll hit a climb that'll put the burn back in your butt. A good mile and a half of uphill, broken briefly by a couple drops with some nice switchbacks toward the top, puts you up in the ranch's higher reaches, surrounded by a stunning panorama.

2.0 From the top of the hill, start down some steep switchbacks, which soon give way to a nice technical section, about 0.5 mile of tight turns through narrow tree gaps and over small boulders. Then you're climbing again, gradually.

3.0 A long, sweeping downhill run turns to a steep, short climb, which leaves you atop a high, windy plateau. Loose singletrack takes you across the top and down the other side.

3.6 Somewhat loose and a bit off-camber, this descent nonetheless offers the opportunity for speed. Long lines turn to longer switchbacks, some of it so close to a slalom course that you expect to be bashing gates with your inside shoulder.

4.2 The end of the descent turns into a fire-road climb, which brings you to a fenceline, the return of the singletrack, and a bit more climbing. Moderate and handleable though the climb may be, the end of it turns steep and mean, with a few well-placed rocks and cacti offering subtle reminders to stay awake.

5.0 A long, bombing downhill the other side of that climb leads to a hard right turn onto some doubletrack. This follows a ridgeline before dumping you left onto some much more technical terrain. Here the big red DANGER signs suddenly appear, warning you of some tricky drops. Heed them.

5.6 A little climbing, a little drop, some more technical moves—this trail keeps it all coming at you. Down here the trail dips toward and away from the creek, hitting some short and steep sections as it works its way through the rolling terrain, using easy climbs to set up roller-coastery downhills.

6.5 Hard-packed doubletrack leads to a fast stretch of descending singletrack.

7.0 Another slalom-style downhill throws you up and down and over another ridge, riding along above an open pasture.

8.0 Beyond the pasture, down to the creek and back up puts you back in the parking lot where you started.

Wolf Mountain Trail

Location: Pedernales Falls State Park, near Johnson City.

Distance: 7.5-mile loop.

Time: 1 hour.

Tread: Mostly doubletrack, with some singletrack.

Aerobic level: Easy to moderate.

Technical difficulty: 2.

Highlights: This wide, easy trail offers some spectacular Hill Country views from the loop on top of Wolf Mountain.

Land status: State Park.

Maps: Free map at park headquarters; USGS Hammett's Crossing.

Access: Take U.S. 290 west from Austin about 35 miles to FM 3232. Turn right and head north about 7 miles. The road into the park jogs slightly to the right. From the park gate, take the main park road down the hill. The trail can be accessed from the primitive camping parking lot.

Notes on the trail: The most important thing to remember while biking the Wolf Mountain Trail is that this is a multiuse trail that gets lots of traffic. Be careful and courteous to hikers, because there will be plenty of them around—especially during the first 2 miles between the trailhead and the primitive camping area. Also, the ride is largely unsheltered, so take necessary precautions in the summertime.

The doubletrack sections that lead you out to the Wolf Mountain loop and back are well marked and smooth, covered with crushed caliche rock. Though it seems easy going, creek crossings provide some leg-pumping climbs, so be prepared. The trail crosses a few creeks before it reaches the primitive camping area, where there are outhouses next to the trail (just in case). After that, traffic lessens and the trail starts winding a little more. Once you pass Jones Spring—a beautiful spot for a breather and a photo or two—you start the ascent to the top of Wolf Mountain. There are some tough rock ledges to get up, and they come at you unexpectedly; again, be prepared. The climb to the top provides the best singletrack out here, which may prompt you to come back down the way you went up. If

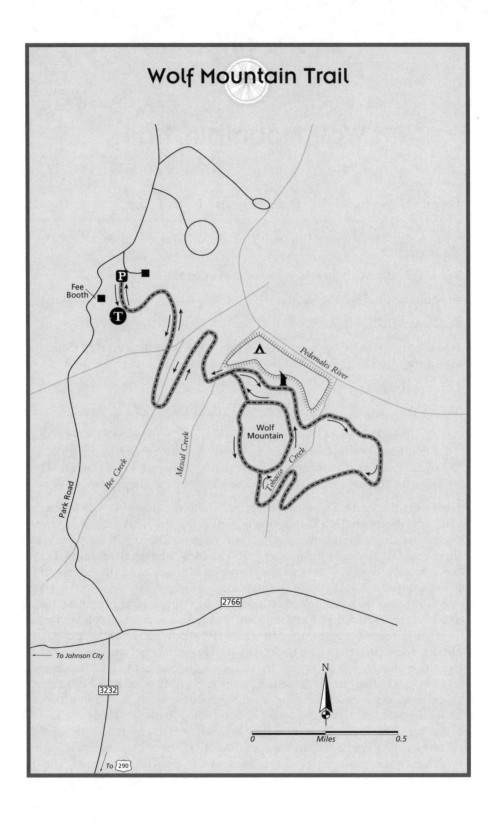

you do, be careful; the ledges are especially treacherous running this direction.

Swimming and camping along the Pedernales River are both exceedingly pleasant, though the park is very crowded on weekends during summer. If you've got the time to hang around, though, you won't be disappointed with a weekend spent at Pedernales Falls.

The Ride

0.0   Trailhead, at parking for primitive camping. The path out from here is wide, hard-packed dirt.

1.1   Bee Creek crossing.

1.5   Here's the first mile marker.

1.7   The primitive camping area begins at the NO CAMPING BELOW ROCK BLUFFS sign. The trail here passes a set of rest rooms, then begins a short climb.

1.9   Mescal Creek crossing; primitive camping area on the left.

2.0   Stay left at the junction, skirting around Wolf Mountain.

2.8   Tobacco Creek crossing.

3.0   Another mile marker.

3.3   At Jones Spring the trail curves right, soon narrowing to rocky singletrack.

3.5   There are a few rock ledges to climb here, so be ready!

3.7   The singletrack begins. As the trail turns upward, it's considerably more difficult than the flat parts at the beginning.

4.0   A steep climb is often blocked by trees here, so watch your head as you grind your way up.

4.5   Mile marker.

4.6   At the intersection of the trail to Butler Mountain, stay to the right to Wolf Mountain.

4.8   When you reach the top, ride the loop the whole way around (starting to the right to follow mile markers). The views of the hill country—especially to the southeast, looking out over Twin Buttes and Lone Mountain—are breathtaking on a clear day.

5.2   At the junction with the trail heading down, turn right. The road down is gravel covered and very fast, and it comes up on the trail junction suddenly, so be aware of hikers on the trail. From there, it's a straight shot back to the trailhead.

5.5   This is the same junction as at 2.0 miles; go left.

6.4   Bee Creek crossing.

7.5   Back at trailhead.

Upper Gorman Creek Trail

Location: Colorado Bend State Park, Bend.

Distance: 7 miles.

Time: 1 hour.

Tread: Mostly doubletrack.

Aerobic level: Moderate.

Technical difficulty: 3.

Highlights: For a fun ride that's friendly to all levels of rider in a gorgeous setting, the Upper Gorman Creek Trail is a tough one to beat. The lay of the land allows for plenty of climbing and descending, all of it manageable by beginning riders in respect to both technical demands and changes in elevation.

Land status: State Park.

Maps: Free map at park headquarters; USGS Bend, Gorman Falls.

Access: From U.S. 183 in Lampasas take FM 580 west 24 miles to Bend. Follow the signs 4 miles to the park entrance. Park headquarters is 6 miles past the entrance on a gravel road, but the parking area for the Upper Gorman Creek Trail is on the right before you get to headquarters.

Notes on the trail: Two separate paths inside Colorado Bend State Park are accessible by bicycle: the River Trail and the Upper Gorman Creek Trail. The River Trail is short, split by the park road, and, frankly, not a whole lot of fun. The Upper Gorman Creek Trail, on the other hand, is two connected loops totaling around 5 miles with an extra mile or so leaving the second loop and heading straight uphill to the park road, all of which offer thoroughly enjoyable riding.

The trails are well marked for the most part, the first loop in blue and the second in yellow. When I rode here, though, the sign indicating the diversion of the loops from the unmarked out-and-back was pretty well hidden. I did the extension sort of by accident. On the way out it's all uphill, though not very difficult. Then you get to bomb down it on the way back! Yet another happy mistake on the bike. After all, isn't that how we usually find the best trails?

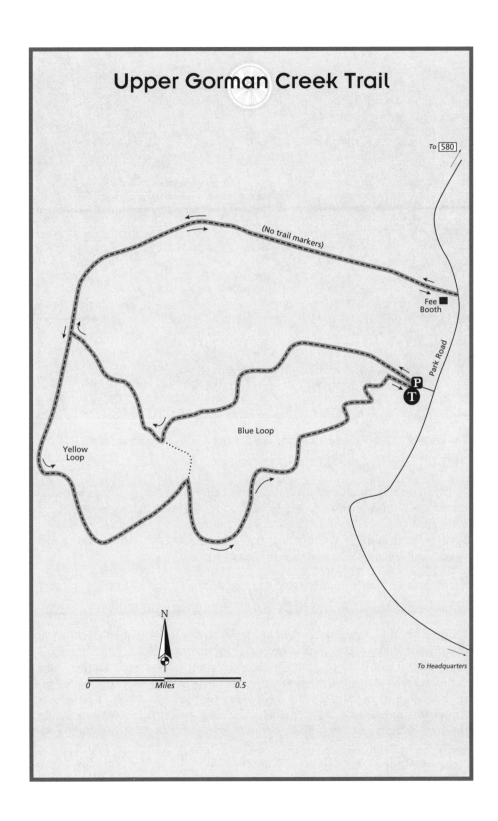

Upper Gorman Creek Trail

To 580

(No trail markers)

Fee
Booth

Park Road

P
T

Blue Loop

Yellow
Loop

N

0   Miles   0.5

To Headquarters

The hills are long and easy at Colorado Bend State Park. Here's a typical scene from the Upper Gorman Creek Trail.

If you do ride the River Trail, remember that it serves mostly as a means for campers and anglers to get to their camping and fishing spots, so be courteous and watch your speed. Also remember that both the Spicewood Springs Trail and the Connecting Trail, which connect either end of the River Trail to the park road, are off limits to bikes.

The Ride

From the parking area along the park road, head out westward on the indicated doubletrack. The trail is not marked for any specific direction, so I randomly selected to go right at the first intersection and do the loops counterclockwise. After the first turn the trail winds its way up a rocky little hillside and turns left into a gorgeous meadow. Through here it continues to climb a little bit along an even, easy grade. After about 0.5 mile the trail flattens out into another grassy meadow that is loaded with wildflowers in spring.

Just past the mile mark is the first junction of the yellow and blue loops. Stay to the right and begin the yellow loop. A few hundred yards up, you'll pass the primitive camping area before you head into a long, gradual downhill. The terrain is smooth enough to allow for considerable speed, but there are some bumps and ruts, so keep your eyes on the trail. It's all doubletrack, which in the absence of any motor traffic turns out to be a pair of wonderful singletracks separated by a high grassy median. It's a good idea to keep to the right and make passing oncoming traffic as easy as possible, especially in the speedy or blind sections.

At about 1.5 miles, past the camping area, be on the watch for a split. The loops will head left, and an extension veers to the right. This trail climbs a long, rocky path up to the park road next to the ranger's residence. It's a nice climb with a great view or two, but at the end you must either turn right onto the road to get back to where you parked or turn around and head back down. I suggest climbing this and heading right back down, as the climb will help warm your legs up and the downhill is worth whatever work it took to get you up here. Back at the main trail, continue straight and you'll find yourself back on the yellow loop heading in the right direction.

Another gradual climb puts you in another nice meadow and leads to another long downhill—yes, it's a pattern. It happens again and again, and it's laid out all but perfectly. At the end of a particularly sustained descent, you'll find that you're back on the blue loop, which is where you want to be. This one dives through the creek bottom and climbs somewhat steeply out of it. Another mile of easy, wandering trail brings you to a final climb and then back to the parking lot.

Good Water Trail

Location: Georgetown.

Distance: 10 miles round-trip.

Time: 1 hour.

Tread: Mix of singletrack and doubletrack.

Aerobic level: Easy.

Technical difficulty: 2.

Highlights: A long, easy ride along Lake Georgetown, the trail connecting Tejas Camp to Russell Park is one for riders of all levels. The trail provides access to a few group camping areas and any number of fishing spots, and odds are you won't see too many other people away from either of the ends.

Land status: The trail and the parks it connects are run by the Fort Worth District of the U.S. Army Corps of Engineers.

Maps: Free map from Tejas Camp or Russell Park; USGS Leander NE.

Access: To start out at Tejas Camp, take U.S. 183 north from TX 29 about 2 miles. Turn right on County Road 258, marked by a small sign. Follow this for about 4.5 miles to Tejas Camp, where CR 258 crosses the north fork of the San Gabriel River, which becomes Lake Georgetown. Park in the Tejas Camp lot and head down the road a tiny bit, cross the river, and take a right at the HIKE TRAIL sign.

Notes on the trail: The Good Water Trail is a 16.6-mile U-shaped trail that goes around the western end of Georgetown Lake. The longer southern half is open to hikers only, but the straighter shot on the northern side is available for biking. Part doubletrack and part singletrack, this out-and-back trail wanders through some very scenic and seldom-ridden terrain along the north fork of the San Gabriel River.

The Ride

From the HIKE TRAIL sign, you'll head out and down along the river, winding through a low shady area, until you take a sharp uphill turn away from the water. The trail is marked with brown stick-figure hiker signs, guiding you through a grassy area and then back across the water again. You'll hit doubletrack at about 0.5 mile; follow the sign to the right and continue on your way.

Much of the trail keeps you exposed, so be sure to use sunscreen and a visor if you can. Now you're in a long, somewhat uneventful though very pretty stretch of trail, loping along some nicely surfaced doubletrack, likely harried by scads of grasshoppers. Deer are as plentiful as the prickly pear along the hard, dry ground of this riverside trail. You'll pass signs showing the way to places like the Cherokee Trailhead and Walnut Camp, and you'll just keep on pedaling.

At about the 4-mile mark, you'll reach the Walnut Camp, and the trail splits. The doubletrack continues straight ahead and comes to a stop when it reaches the water. The singletrack that leads left climbs up and through a rocky section of hilly terrain, the first mountain-bikey mountain biking you'll do out here. Eventually, after many tight and rocky twists and turns, the trail leads out into the parking area at Russell Park. This is the end of the line—time to turn around and head back. The way down is considerably more treacherous than the way up, as you're descending many series of rock ledges and quick drops. Be careful. And have a nice ride back.

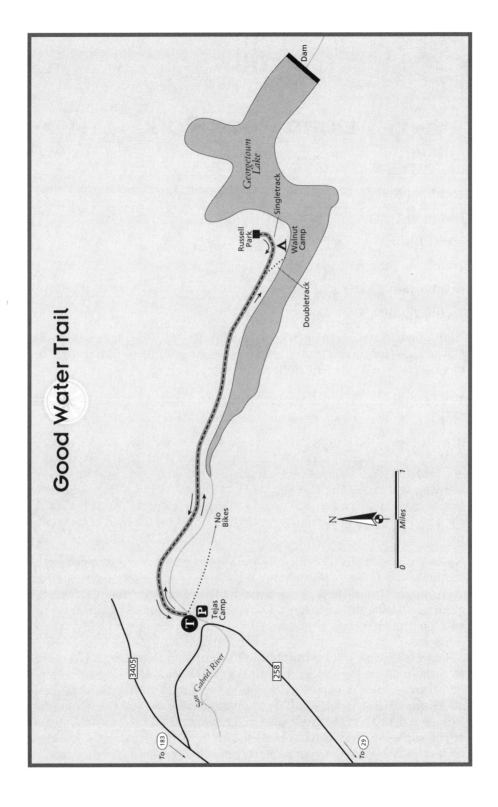

Good Water Trail

Georgetown Lake

Dam

Singletrack

Russell Park

Walnut Camp

Doubletrack

No Bikes

Tejas Camp

San Gabriel River

3405

258

To 183

To 29

N

Miles
0   1

Dana Peak Park

Location: Nolanville, between Temple and Killeen.

Distance: 7 miles.

Time: 1 hour.

Tread: Mostly singletrack, some doubletrack.

Aerobic level: Moderate.

Technical difficulty: 3.

Highlights: Conquerable though technically challenging singletrack, killer views from atop Dana Peak, and surprisingly little trail traffic make this Central Texas ride an extremely pleasant surprise.

Land status: Federal Park, U.S. Army Corps of Engineers.

Maps: Free map at park headquarters; USGS Killeen and Nolanville.

Access: From I–35 south of Temple, take U.S. 190 west for 5 miles toward Killeen. Exit at Simmons Road—Stillhouse Hollow Park (two exits *past* the exit for Stillhouse Hollow Dam), turning left at the stop, passing under the highway, and taking the first right, FM 2410. Follow this about 6 miles to Comanche Gap Road, turn left, and head toward the park. Instead of going all the way in, park in the open area on the left side of the road at the sharp right turn (the turn is marked with a sign). The trail heads out from here.

Notes on the trail: Though this trail often seems a maze, laced with shortcuts and crisscrosses as numerous as the cacti, there's not enough space to get truly lost, and the main trails are for the most part distinguishable. Using the fencelines, Dana Peak, and Stillhouse Lake as reference points, you can find your way to and through each section with few problems.

Dana Peak Park is a beautiful little piece of land that sees its fair share of fisherfolk and picnickers, but it's still relatively unknown—and unmarked—when it comes to biking the trails. With a little organized effort, the existing trails could be connected and marked for a fantastic loop, and the rest of the land could be protected from the inevitable damage of unchecked trail extension. As it stands, the main paths are just better worn than the outlaw paths, so stay on the big ones.

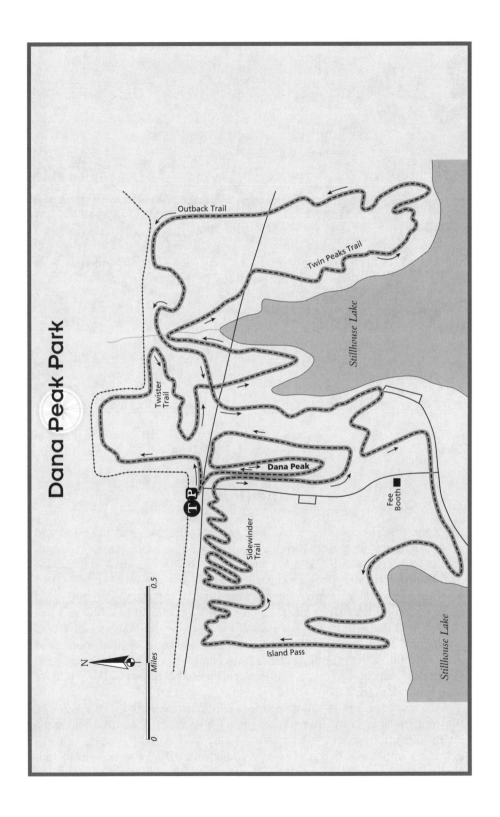

Dana Peak Park

Outback Trail

Twin Peaks Trail

Twister Trail

Stillhouse Lake

Dana Peak

Sidewinder Trail

Fee Booth

Island Pass

Stillhouse Lake

TP

N

Miles

0   0.5

High atop Dana Peak. It's a straight drop down from here. There aren't many hills in Dana Peak Park, but the few that are here are not to be trifled with.

The Ride

From the roadside parking area, head out past the gate and fire road and go left along the fenceline. It quickly turns to singletrack, somewhat hoof-pocked, winding along the fenceline a ways before taking a sharp right turn into the Twister Trail. Eventually this dumps you into an open field where many paths crisscross each other. Stick to the main one and you'll come to some rocky singletrack down near the lake. Mild climbs and lots of fast, hard dirt will bring you around the point of the lake and eastward toward the Twin Peaks Trail. The names of these trails are not marked as such, and the signs that are out here are somewhat hard to follow, so get the park's map and just use the landmarks of the lake and the peaks to keep you oriented.

A bit past the 3-mile mark, heading southeast near the lake's shore, a shortcut trail heads off to your left. The Twin Peaks Trail area has some tough hills and somewhat nasty steps along with a big natural ramp—all crammed into some fast and windy singletrack. If you're not up to that challenge, take the shortcut. It feeds you back into the main trail not too far after all that stuff. From there it's a cruise along the Outback Trail back to the fenceline, where you'll turn left and head back toward the lagoon area. This section is fun and fast, but after you pass the creek and approach the fire road, it can get a little confusing. Best to get on the fire road, hang a right, and follow this for just a couple hundred yards until you see the trail break off again to the left. (If you do get offtrack, it won't be too long before you see more enticing singletrack, so don't worry too much, just ride.)

In this area southwest of the lake, all sorts of fantastic trail feeds on and off the fire road and the main park road—depending on conditions. When I rode here there had been some recent rain, and the section down near the western tip of the lake was totally flooded. Two oldsters in an aluminum fishing boat were drowning a good bit of bait right about where I wanted to be riding. Needless to say, my bike, my spandex, and I got some awfully funny looks. I waded back up through the grass to the park road and backtracked a bit, back around past the entrance and west on the main road until I could get onto the Sidewinder Trail. This likely will not be necessary for you; you should be able to access the Sidewinder Trail— definitely a part of the park you don't want to miss—after tooling around past the lake and across the dead-straight Island Pass. The Sidewinder Trail coils and swings you back eastward just inside the main road until a bridge takes you across the park road.

Now there's some back and forth around the perimeter of Dana Peak, following a clear-cut path, until eventually the trail takes a turn straight up to the top of the hill. After taking in the fantastic view afforded by this lookout position, be *very* careful on the way back down. It's somewhat loose and rocky—and almost as near a straight drop as you'd want to take on. At the bottom it's a straight shot back out to the parking area outside the park.

BLORA/Fort Hood Trailblazers Mountain Bike Park

Location: On Belton Lake, in Fort Hood.

Distance: 8.5-mile loop.

Time: 1.5 hours.

Tread: Mostly singletrack.

Aerobic level: Moderate to strenuous.

Technical difficulty: 4.

Highlights: Fast singletrack with some long, tricky, speedy descents and leg-burning climbs to match. This trail is exclusively for mountain bikes.

Land status: Part of the Belton Lake Outdoor Recreation Area. The mountain bike trails are administered by the Fort Hood Trailblazers Mountain Bike Club. Fees apply.

Maps: Map available at BLORA administration building, at the main entrance; USGS Nolanville, Bland.

Access: From I–35 in Belton, take TX 190 west to Loop 121. Go north on Loop 121 to Sparta Road and turn left. Follow this 7.5 miles past FM 439 to the BLORA entrance. A sign on the left marks the gravel road to the trailhead. Bikers must register at the main office, about 0.25 mile past the sign.

Notes on the trail: This trail lies within the boundaries of the Belton Lake Outdoor Recreation Area, a veritable Eden of outdoor activity—not least of which is mountain biking. The 8.5-mile intermediate loop is complemented by a 4-mile novice trail with very little elevation change, as well as a very short and easy children's trail. So there is riding out here for everyone, from the consummate hammerhead to the training-wheeled first-timer.

The 8.5-mile intermediate loop is a fast and challenging trail that offers lightning-fast singletrack winding flat and smooth through thick stands of cedar as well as long, snaking climbs and boulder-strewn technical drops

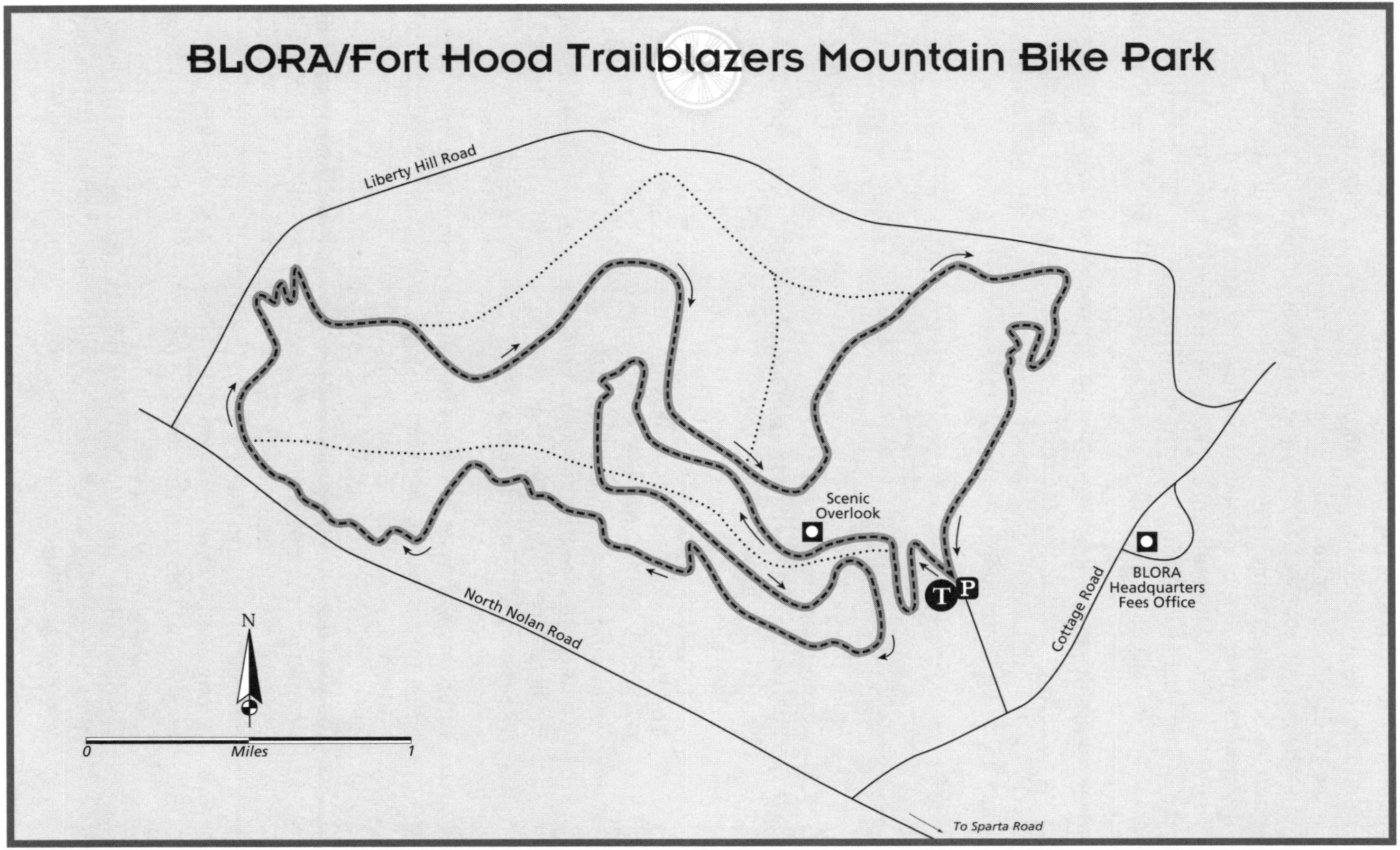

BLORA/Fort Hood Trailblazers Mountain Bike Park

Liberty Hill Road

Scenic Overlook

BLORA Headquarters Fees Office

Cottage Road

North Nolan Road

To Sparta Road

N

Miles

0   1

that will have your back tire brushing your bottom on more than one occasion. The trail is incredibly well marked at every junction or turn, with three colors of arrows marking novice, intermediate, and expert routes. The opening stretches offer a nice warm-up of relatively flat singletrack that winds through some often thickly forested areas before dropping you down a 100-plus-foot bluff, then bringing you back up, and back down, and so on. The climbs are interspersed with enough singletrack to keep them from being too tiring, so you can afford to go all out here. Any treacherous descents are well marked as well, with bright red DANGER! flags in full view.

By the way, that's not thunder you're hearing out there—it's some heavy artillery sounding off at Fort Hood, which lies just to the north. The Fort Hood Trailblazers are responsible for this mountain bike trail, and they are to be commended for the job they've done.

The Ride

0.0 From the parking lot, the trail begins down the fenceline in the direction opposite the main road.

0.7 First split; the novice trail breaks from the intermediate and expert trails here.

1.2 A steep shortcut to the ridge trail breaks to the right, and the main loop continues forward.

1.7 The first stretch of this trail is fun, flat, winding singletrack; it continues awhile after this spot. This is the first junction of the novice and intermediate/expert trails.

3.2 When the novice trail breaks left at a jeep road crossing, the intermediate/expert trail continues on the go-kart–style singletrack. The trail splits are well marked, but there are a number of them, so watch out.

3.7 After this jeep road crossing, follow the intermediate trail to the left and down into another wooded area. Some winding trail brings you to a steep, technical climb.

4.5 Attention! This steep downhill is marked with DANGER signs, and for good reason. While all the *dangerous* areas are ridable, they all deserve your utmost respect. The best line on this one is marked with arrows, and though the drop gets steep, it is manageable and fun. And, of course, there's a nice steep climb at the end.

5.4 A long climb turns immediately into a steep drop, marked DANGER once again. This one's steeper and faster than the last one, so keep firm control of your speed.

5.9 The trail hits a fire road that goes long and fast on a slight downhill grade, leading you through a shady, wooded area and then out into a large clearing that offers a great view of Belton Lake.

7.3   A long stretch of very fast and fun singletrack again breaks out of the woods by the lake. Some whoop-de-dos and curvy singletrack follow that let you use momentum to fly over everything.

7.6   Then comes a series of super-steep climbs and drops, with DANGER markers aplenty. This is pretty much the end of the fun; a long, brutal climb back up to the top of the park follows—about 200 feet of gain in less than 0.5 mile.

8.4   Back at the parking lot and picnic area. The trail is marked further, taking you down the fenceline and out into the road for a nice cool-down loop.

Walnut Creek

Location: Austin.

Distance: About 7 miles total.

Time: 1 hour.

Tread: Mix of singletrack and doubletrack.

Aerobic level: Easy to moderate.

Technical difficulty: 2 to 3.

Highlights: A veritable maze of crisscrossing singletrack spreading out from another maze of doubletrack, this city park offers endless opportunities to get out and spin your wheels. Walnut Creek is a popular North Austin park that has remained something of a secret to mountain bikers, but a map on the Internet (interpreted here) and an ongoing effort by some locals to mark trails and block outlaw extensions is making it more orderly and more fun to ride, and thus a more popular destination.

Land status: City Park.

Maps: Free map from Austin Area Christian Mountain Bikers on groups.yahoo.com/group/aacmb; USGS Austin East.

Access: In Austin, take Lamar Boulevard north past U.S. 183 for a few miles to the park entrance on the left. Proceed on the park road to the parking area by the swimming pool. The trail begins right behind the lot.

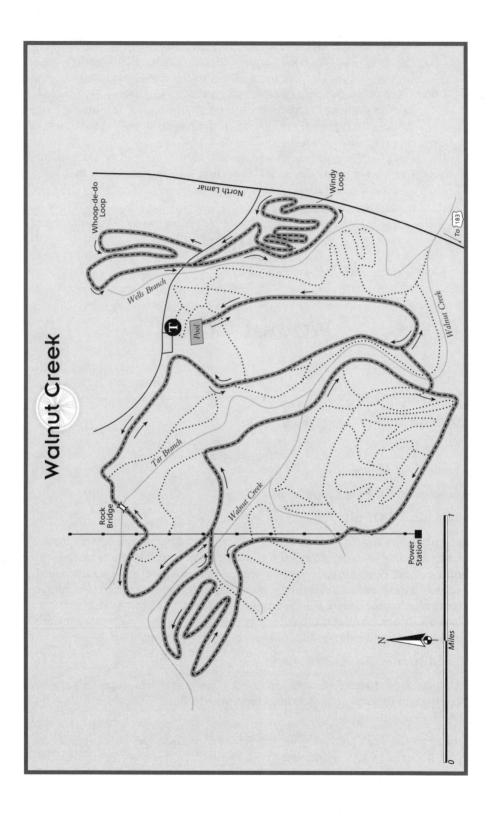

Walnut Creek

Whoop-de-do Loop

North Lamar

Windy Loop

To 183

Wells Branch

Pool

T

Tar Branch

Rock Bridge

Walnut Creek

Walnut Creek

Power Station

N

Miles

0   1

Notes on the trail: There has been an effort recently to put the trails of Walnut Creek in order. The park contains a big jumble of singletrack upon singletrack cutting across one another and swooping every which way on the banks of Walnut Creek and its Tar and Wells Branches. It's obvious that there are too many paths for the small amount of land to sustain and remain healthy. When the trails are clear and orderly, especially in a city park of this size, everyone benefits, so kudos to those who are attempting to cut things back to a reasonable state.

The park is divided by Walnut Creek and two of its branches, the Tar Branch and the Wells Branch. The main trail basically traces the banks of each of these, winding along one and then curving over to another, tracing its route, crossing, and working its way over to the third. Over and among these routes, many singletrack paths generally leave the main trail, descend the creek banks, and then climb back out to rejoin the main trail.

Most of the trails here are fairly easy. A beginning rider could manage the main trail pretty much the whole way around, though some of the side paths that drop to the creekbeds can get pretty steep without warning. You may want to check them out before diving blindly down any of them.

As you'll notice when you park your vehicle, there is a swimming pool here. While not as good as a swimming hole hidden in the woods, it's still a nice place to cool off after a ride. It does get crowded, though—much like the rest of the park. Still, most visitors are of the swimming and picnicking varieties, so even when the park is crowded, you'll still ride some fairly long stretches of trail without seeing anyone else.

The Ride

The trails at Walnut Creek can be roughly divided into two sections. The majority of the miles here are west of the park road and consist of a main trail that's either doubletrack or a wide single path that follows all three segments of Walnut Creek and an endless array of pieces of singletrack that dart off the main trail down the creek banks and then climb back up to meet the main trail again. This main trail is a continuous set of long, fairly straight avenues connected at both ends to those tracing its opposite banks and those of the neighboring branches.

The other, smaller section of the park consists of two very clearly marked 1-mile loops of challenging singletrack that straddle the park road near where it meets Lamar Boulevard—both to the east of Wells Branch. Both of these are a blast—tight and twisty singletrack that bounds up and down quick, steep hills, with banked corners and ramps popping up often in the middle of the trail. If you grew up on BMX, you'll feel like a kid again on these two loops.

On most of my rides here I've started out at the parking lot by the pool and headed out past the NO MOTORIZED VEHICLES sign, down the hill toward the creek. One circuit of the main trail, while diverging on the better-traveled pieces of singletrack, turns out to be about 5.5 miles by the time you're back at the beginning. You'll have to cross the creek a couple times, and you'll want to be sure to include the segment beyond the rock bridge that travels under the power lines running from a maintenance shed to a power station. This is an all-out wide-open sprint that leads back to the original section of main trail.

Once you're back at this part of the main trail, head back toward the parking lot and turn right when you get to the road. Follow the road over the bridge to the singletrack that runs alongside. This is the Windy Loop and should be marked with a MAIN TRAIL sign; follow it until it turns a hard right down into the woods. This is the first 1-mile loop, a long and fast series of trips to the creek and back that eventually bring you back to the road where you began. A left at the road or at the trail parallel to the road brings you back toward the bridge. Just before the bridge, the second 1-mile loop leaves the road off to the right. This is the Whoop-de-do Loop, and it lives up to its name—plenty of chances to get air between your tires and the ground on this one.

More than likely, you'll turn back and repeat these two loops a couple times each before calling it a day, at which point you'll take the road over the bridge and back to the pool parking lot on the left.

Emma Long Motocross Park
(City Park)

Location: Austin.

Distance: 6.2 miles.

Time: 1 hour.

Tread: All singletrack.

Aerobic level: Strenuous.

Technical difficulty: 5.

Highlights: This is the closest thing to freeriding I've found in Texas. A relentless series of steep drops and climbs with plenty of technical maneuvering in between, City Park, as it's called by the locals, rewards hard work and perseverance with an adrenaline-packed ride—and punishes the lazy or disrespectful with a barrage of nasty endos. Be careful out there.

Land status: City Park.

Maps: Free map at the trailhead (though the box is usually empty); USGS Austin West.

Access: Take FM 2222 west from Loop 360 to City Park Road, the first stoplight, and turn left. Follow this winding road for about 4 miles to Oak Shores Drive. Turn left and follow the winding road about 1 mile to the parking area on the left. The trailhead is directly ahead of you on the way in, just past the donation box and the sign.

Notes on the trail: As the name suggests, this place is primarily a motocross course, though on any given day (except for motorace days) the rigs with pedals will outnumber those with throttles. The trail is very steep and fast, traversing countless limestone ledges, up and down and up and down, skating along ridgelines and bombing through gulleys. The most important skill a rider can have out here is the one that lets you slide your butt off the back of the saddle and maintain control while dropping off rock tables that'll test the limits of your suspension—and your nerves. Be careful, be careful, have fun, and be careful.

Emma Long Motocross Park (City Park)

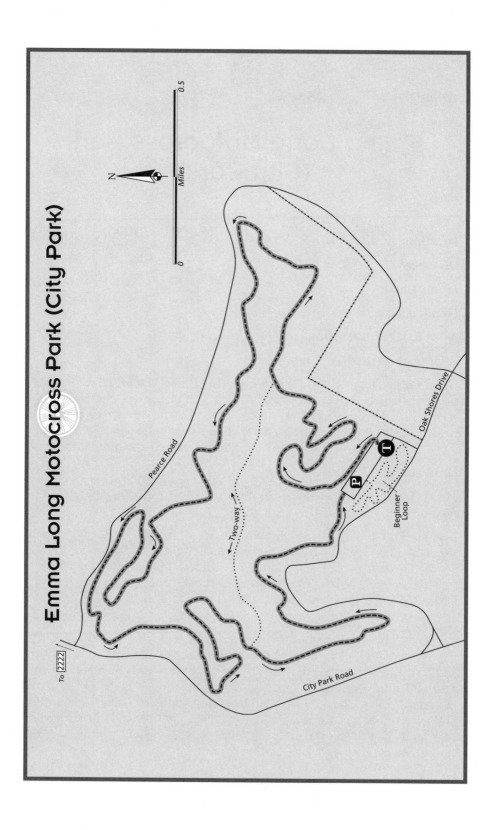

Bring your climbing legs to City Park, because this place doesn't take kindly to lollygaggers.

The Ride

0.0   The trailhead is clearly marked at the corner of the L-shaped entry/parking area. The entry point is the very first ledge, and like the sign says, it gives you a good idea of what to expect. Here as elsewhere on the trail, get your momentum and your front wheel up, and let your bike flow over the rise.

0.25   After a bit of pleasantly rolling singletrack, hit the first steep climb, quick but tough. This is followed shortly by another tough, quick climb.

0.8   This is the first serious drop. It comes in two sections—a steep swervy hill followed by a series of limestone shelves. Watch the sharp right at the bottom.

1.3   Start a nice technical climb up some winding, rock-studded trail for about 0.5 mile. After the crest, the trail dips down briefly, then heads back up again.

2.0   The climb ends—that last 0.8 mile surely felt like much more. But now, the downhill! Follow the curve to the left (there's a bench for a rest if you like), and start the descent. It's speedy and over too fast, and then you start another climb.

2.3   Partway up this climb there's a big ol' sign that reads TRAIL CLOSED. Because of unapproved cutting of vegetation, the Austin parks department has closed this section of trail for a ten-year growth period, to reopen in January 2009. Heed the warning, and be sensible. Do not cut trail or damage vegetation. Head to the left past the sign and keep climbing, just another couple hundred yards or so. Some of these ledges will chew up your big ring if you don't hit them just right (mine looks like a hockey player's mouth), so watch out.

2.8   Reach the top of that climb, followed by some big steps going down. Don't forget to peel your eyes from directly in front of your front tire and watch for the MAIN TRAIL signs. Mostly it's easy to follow, but there are a few spots around here where you can get off track.

3.3   Head up another long, rocky climb. Some mild ups and downs and a fairly long flat section follow.

4.1   The trail runs along City Park Road here and then turns into a long downhill, ending at a tiny bridge traversing the creek. Some nice shady singletrack then takes you to another big climb chock-full of boulders. If you've been working on that nifty J-hop move, this trail is a good place to practice it. It makes cleaning these ledges much easier.

4.7   Another of the tougher drops. Take care.

5.5 Here's the last of the tough ones. Hold your line and get your butt back. The trail then heads down below trailhead level on a long speedy descent and takes you back up a wide trough.

6.2 Back in the parking lot. Breathe for a minute, and then get out there for another lap!

Town Lake Hike and Bike

Location: Austin.

Distance: 10 miles round trip.

Time: 1 hour.

Tread: Mostly wide, crushed limestone path; some street.

Aerobic level: Easy.

Technical difficulty: 1.

Highlights: Not a mountain bike trail as much as a multipurpose hike and bike path, the Town Lake Trail is nonetheless a ride that anyone stopping in Austin ought to check out. The path runs along the banks of Town Lake, a part of the Colorado River, traveling through Zilker Park and passing the Auditorium Shores concert area, an imposing statue of local deity Stevie Ray Vaughn, and numerous other parks and recreational spaces in a loop from west to east and back again.

Land status: City Park.

Maps: Map available on-line at www.txinfo.com; USGS Austin West, Austin East.

Access: You can access the Town Lake Trail from any number of places along the lake in Austin. One of the bigger parking areas is next to Auditorium Shores on the south side of the lake. Exit I–35 at Riverside and head west. Turn right into the parking area just past South First Street. The mileage markers start here, moving around the trail counterclockwise.

Notes on the trail: A ride around the Town Lake Hike and Bike should be undertaken more for the purpose of getting a look at the city of Austin

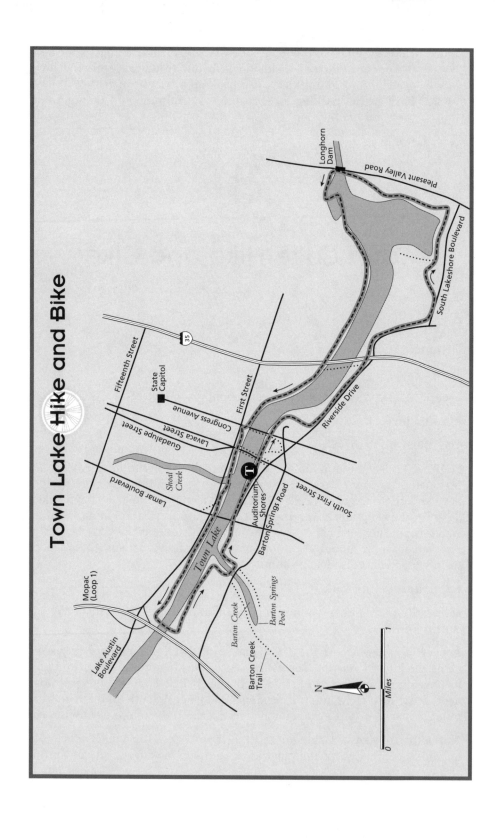

Town Lake Hike and Bike

than for getting in any serious bike riding. This slow-moving, peaceful path is heavily used by walkers and joggers and their dogs and kids, often moving along three to four abreast. Be patient and move carefully; that's what this trail is all about.

There are tremendous views of the city skyline and of other parts of town from either side of the lake, making for a remarkably placid setting in the middle of town. Local treasures such as the statue of Stevie Ray Vaughn just west of the Auditorium Shores parking area and the Zilker Zephyr, a miniature train that runs through Zilker Park along the trail, are just a couple of the things that can capture your interest on the way.

The Ride

Most of the Town Lake Trail is a wide, crushed limestone path that accommodates a good deal of traffic comfortably—which is good, because this trail sees plenty of traffic. Remember to call out your approach to walkers and runners you pass. A simple "On your left" works wonders for biker PR.

There are a few things to watch out for: The trail divides as it approaches each bridge along the way—at Lamar, South First, Congress, and I–35. If continuing past any of these on the trail, stay to the left at the split, closer to the water. Makes sense, right? The Mopac Footbridge and Longhorn Dam, at either end of the path, are more straightforward.

Also, as you pass the Austin American Statesman building heading east from Congress, the trail breaks off to the right, becoming no longer a trail and following Riverside Drive on a wide sidewalk. It continues this way past I–35 (be *very careful* crossing I–35) and all the way to the Colorado River Park on South Lakeshore Boulevard. The rest of the way is trail.

Barton Creek Greenbelt

Location: Austin.

Distance: 15-mile loop.

Time: 2 hours.

Tread: Mostly singletrack, some wide path.

Aerobic level: Moderate.

Technical difficulty: 3.

Highlights: A long, forested ride along the banks of Barton Creek through the middle of Austin, the Greenbelt Trail has something for everyone. The main trail is an enjoyable trek for beginners and experts alike, and numerous side trails and extensions allow for practically endless opportunities to lengthen and enhance your ride.

Land status: City Park.

Maps: Map available on-line at www.txinfo.com; USGS Austin West, Austin East.

Access: There are seven official access points for the Barton Creek Greenbelt, but the ones most used for biking it are Zilker Park and Loop 360. For Zilker Park, which marks the beginning of the trail, take I–35 to Austin and exit Riverside, heading west. Follow this past Congress Avenue to Barton Springs Road and turn left. Take Barton Springs Road past Lamar, past the next stoplight, to the Zilker Park entrance on your left. Follow the park road to the main parking lot by Barton Springs (the pool). The trail heads out from the far west end of the lot. For the Loop 360 access, continue on Barton Springs Road past the park to Mopac (Loop 1). Head south on Mopac to the left exit for Loop 360 (or Capital of Texas Highway) south. Merge left, and turn left at the first stoplight. The parking area is on your left.

Notes on the trail: This is it. This is the trail at the heart of mountain biking in Texas. Everyone has his or her own favorite trail, but this one—in the center of the capital city in the center of the state—is all things to all people, bringing pleasure to all who attempt it and endless discovery and enjoyment to any who dig a little deeper. Scoffed at by some unknowing

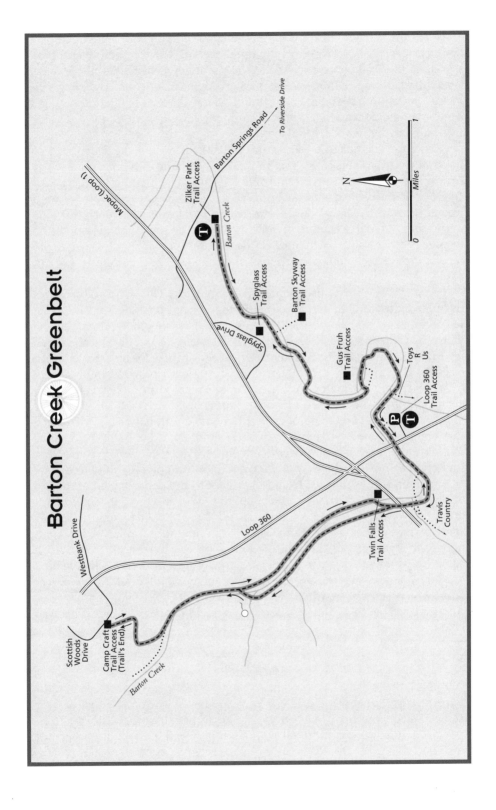

Barton Creek Greenbelt

Mopac (Loop 1)

To Riverside Drive

Barton Springs Road

Zilker Park
Trail Access

Barton Creek

Spyglass
Trail Access

Barton Skyway
Trail Access

Spyglass Drive

Gus Fruh
Trail Access

Toys
R
Us

Loop 360
Trail Access

Travis
Country

Westbank Drive

Loop 360

Twin Falls
Trail Access

Scottish
Woods
Drive

Camp Craft
Trail Access
(Trail's End)

Barton Creek

N

Miles

0   1

elitists as the "Greenbahn" for the flatness of the main path and worshiped by those familiar with its very hilly outer regions, the true nature and best secrets of the trail come only with time spent exploring. Its trails provide year-round biking, running, and hiking opportunities, and when we're lucky enough to have a creekbed full of water, the trail is the outdoor epicenter of Austin, drawing droves of swimmers to slack on its rocky banks. It is an amazing, wonderful place.

Heavy use has taken a toll on the trails. Erosion left the Zilker end of the trail so rutted and rocky that in 2001–02 the first 1.5 miles underwent severe reconstructive surgery, turning it from abused and widened rocky singletrack to a raked and steamrolled avenue so wide you can drive a tractor down it. A change for the worse, I'd say, but it does make this part of the trail accessible to more people. It used to be rough going both in the technical aspect and the bone-shaking aspect, but no more. Beyond the second crossing, though, alterations have been kept to a minimum—so far, at least.

The majority of trail users enter at Zilker Park. This starting point has the added attraction of access to the Barton Springs pool, a gigantic spring-fed swimming hole set across Barton Creek that is as integral part of the identity of Austin as the Greenbelt itself. At a year-round 68°F, if the creek isn't flowing along the trail, you can't beat the springs for a postride swim.

Getting on the trail at the Loop 360 access lets you avoid the majority of those people getting on at Zilker. There's less traffic here, making it a good option for people who load up the car and drive to the trailhead. Wherever you get on, remember that the entire trail is two-way, meaning that someone could be coming at you around every bend. There are lots of kids and dogs that don't react to oncoming cycles so quickly, so be careful—and be courteous. Call out when you pass, and always yield to hikers.

The main trail is marked from Zilker Park to the opposite end at the top of the Hill of Life, a grueling, rocky climb that meets the outside world at Scottish Woods Trail in a subdivision off Loop 360. I've described this route as an out-and-back below. There are many more miles of trails out here, and I've marked the mileage points on the main trail from which some extensions diverge and provided a brief description of them. There are many others, though a good number of those turn outlaw sooner or later. My best advice would be to explore, but heed signs and fences. Above all, respect the trails as they are, and do not cut new ones. This trail belongs to everyone.

The Ride

0.0   Zilker Park trailhead. The trail starts out as a wide and flattened hike-and-bike-style path running parallel to the north bank of Barton Creek. There's lots of runner, hiker, and dog traffic for the first

1.5 miles, so keep your speed reasonable and your bike under control, no matter how tempting it may be to do otherwise.

1.0 Here's a little bit of a hill. The side trail to Campbell's Hole, the most popular swimming spot on Barton Creek, cuts through the cedar on your left at the first hill, about 1 mile in.

1.2 The Barton Skyway access feeds into the main trail from the opposite side of the creek. A few yards after that, the Spyglass Trail access hits on the north side of the creek, next to a pair of rest rooms. After climbing that small hill, the trail more closely resembles singletrack.

1.5 First creek crossing. In dry times you can sail through this 30-yard trough in a middle gear, pedaling hard to keep upright in the deep gravel. In wetter days, however, you could be wading through belly-deep water rushing cold against your tender parts.

1.7 Second creek crossing. This one never gets too deep, but it does move quickly, so be careful wading through water. If it's dry, you've got a little limestone ledge to pop up onto and then a short, steep hill to get up. Get in the right gear and hit it. The trail bends sharply left at the top.

2.1 The Gus Fruh access hits the creek on the other bank.

2.4 Third creek crossing. You have a choice here: A sharp left after a short wooden trail reinforcement takes you up a quick hill, or keep straight and ride some lunar-looking water-shaped rocks, eventually bearing left and twisting back through some tight and rocky singletrack to meet the other split. Both of these usually hold little to no water.

2.6 Fourth creek crossing. There's not usually much water here either, and chances are you won't even realize it's a crossing. The singletrack after this is flat and fast, a good smooth surface with wide turns that begs for a sprint. Watch for oncoming traffic.

3.2 Fifth creek crossing. This one's wide and shallow. If the water's moving, it's usually moving fast. If it's dry, this is a challenging ride through a long stretch of loose gravel and big boulders, an obstacle course that you'll be eager to get through without touching a toe to the ground. On the other side, the main trail takes a right turn. A trail that keeps going straight before this turn leads to a huge network of unmarked trails that locals call the Toys R Us hill (since the back lot of a Toys R Us is at the very top). There are any number of ways to get up and then back down this hill, which will eventually return you to the main trail about 0.25 mile from where you left it.

3.7 Loop 360 access. The mulched path that winds uphill to the left leads out to the Loop 360 parking lot. Continue straight here, passing under the overpass. Again, watch for traffic.

3.9 Nice climb here, leading to a long piece of singletrack that keeps along the edge of a ridge, eventually diving down a fairly steep and somewhat sketchy drop. A pedestrian-only trail veers away from this route just before the climb and rejoins it just after the drop.

4.3   Sixth creek crossing. This one's optional. The trail along the creek's southern bank gets narrow and rocky, sticking to a steep rock wall. Much of it is not ridable, and a short piece requires that you shoulder your rig and walk, holding a chain anchored into the rock. Crossing gives you a short blast of singletrack that ends in a rock garden that'll test your balance and technical skills. When this crossing's full of water, though, it's the deepest one out here, often coming chest high on my 5 feet and 11 inches. If there's no water, you definitely want to cross.

4.5   Seventh creek crossing. If you didn't cross at the last one, you don't have to worry about this one. Just keep going straight. If you did cross, then cross back here. Water won't be more than midthigh high, and dry times make it a sprint through a wide gravel bed. On the southern side of the creek again, there is another departure point. The set of trails known as Travis Country (for the residential area they eventually end up in) begins here, heading out to the west. There are lots of trails here, too, but a main route brings you out and over a series of tough, technical climbs and descents, eventually dumping you out near Southwest Parkway. A right turn at the street and short ride through the neighborhood gets you back on the trail either just past a water treatment center or, farther along, at neighborhood's end—either route offering a long and mostly downhill run back to the main trail, a little over a mile upstream from the starting point. This is a tough trail; attempt it with caution. It's completely unmarked, too.

4.6   Eighth creek crossing. Just after passing under the Mopac overpass, you can cross the creek at this wide, rocky spot, or you can keep straight. The Twin Falls access is on the other side of the creek. From here out to the spring, about 1.5 miles ahead, trails run along both banks of the creek, so you can ride out on one side and back on the other. I recommend staying put here and riding the other side on the way back. It's fast, narrow singletrack on this side. Watch out—a barbed-wire fence runs very close to your left side for much of the way.

5.1   Twin Falls, the second most popular swimming hole out here, is named for the pair of low waterfalls that cut through a large slab of wide-open rock. Loaded with sunbathing, beer-drinking, time-wasting folks of all kinds when it's warm and the water's running, this is a great spot to take a dip and cool down and watch the local freaks make merry. The trail beyond here is fast and has a few technical challenges involving quick bursts of rock climbing and requiring some pretty good balance.

6.1 Ninth creek crossing. A spring bubbles out of the rocks on your left just past the crossing point at the end of the trail on this side. There are a couple places where you can cross, but it's deeper closer to the spring. On the other side, turn left and keep heading out. It's mostly wide gravel path from here to the end.

6.3 Sculpture Falls is on your left, a lesser-used swimming hole that's not quite as easy to get to.

7.0 The Hill of Life. You'll hate it, you'll love it. Get into a small gear and pedal away, eyes out front and pinned to a line, gaining more than 300 feet in a third of a mile. It'll feel longer and higher. At the top, turn around and head back down. There's some unmarked singletrack that makes the descent more fun, accessed about two-thirds of the way up on the left (or the right on the way down).

7.3 Camp Craft access or Trail's End access. Get a breath before heading back down.

8.6 Back at the ninth creek crossing, keep to this side and go straight, making your way down from the wide gravel path to the creekside singletrack. The way from here back to Mopac overpass is perhaps the most fun you'll have out here, fast and twisty singletrack with a few tough spots.

10.1 At the Mopac overpass, cross the creek. It's slippery here when the water's running—and when it's not. Be careful if you ride it. Turn left at the other side.

10.2 Cross again if you like; the chain section is ahead.

10.4 Cross back if you did cross previously.

11.0 Loop 360 access is on your right.

11.4 This is the fifth creek crossing on the way out.

12.1 Next crossing, followed closely by the crossing closest to Gus Fruh.

12.5 Gus Fruh access is on your right.

12.9 Turn right, head down, and cross again. Be careful heading down that rock—it's quite a drop-off into the creekbed's gravel.

13.1 Last crossing. The rest of the trail is smooth sailing.

14.6 Back at the Zilker trailhead.

Homestead Trail

Location: Austin.

Distance: 4 miles.

Time: 30 minutes.

Tread: Mix of singletrack and doubletrack.

Aerobic level: Easy.

Technical difficulty: 1.

Me and the Mrs. out for a Sunday ride in our favorite park. Cathy makes quick work of the Homestead Trail.

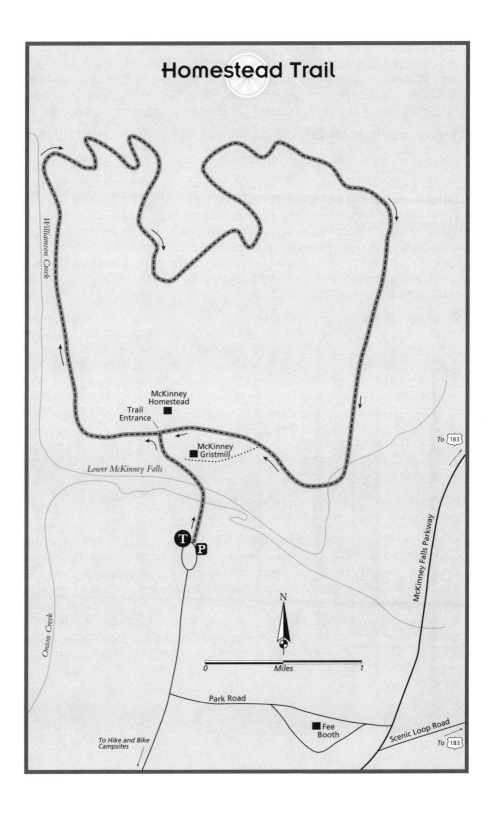

Homestead Trail

Williamson Creek

McKinney
Homestead

Trail
Entrance

McKinney
Gristmill

Lower McKinney Falls

Onion Creek

T

P

To 183

McKinney Falls Parkway

N

0   Miles   1

Park Road

Fee
Booth

Scenic Loop Road

To 183

To Hike and Bike
Campsites

Highlights: A gorgeous, winding, wooded singletrack loop on the south-eastern outskirts of Austin, the Old Homestead Trail offers a fun ride as well as an educational look at the ruins of the old McKinney homestead. A 5-mile paved trail running through the park, the Onion Creek Hike and Bike Trail, has a nice dirt diversion just south of the primitive camp area.

Land status: State Park.

Maps: Free park map; USGS Montopolis.

Access: From I–35, take U.S. 71 east to U.S. 183 south. After a couple miles, turn right onto McKinney Falls Parkway, just past the sign for the park. The park entrance is just a few miles up on the right. Past park head-quarters take the first right and park in the lot at the end of the road. A trail heads out from here to the limestone bed surrounding Williamson Creek. Cross the creek—which could be anything from bone-dry to a genuine flowing creek—and head up into the trees on the other side at the trailhead sign.

Notes on the trail: Though short and pretty easy, this nice little nugget of singletrack offers fun for riders of all ages and skill levels. Hard-packed dirt winds through dense groves of cedar and oak that are also a popular stop on the migratory route of the painted bunting. Sure, birding and biking are tough to do at the same time, but nothing says you can't stop and just sit still once in a while!

Don't get too lulled out here—there are a few short, steep drops and climbs with some roots running across them, and there are plenty of close-hanging tree branches that would like to say hello to your head. There are plenty of tight corners to test your handling skills, too.

The Ride

After crossing the falls, head up a quick hill at the trail sign and turn left. The ruins of the McKinney homestead are on your immediate right, and the trail goes out clockwise from here. About halfway around, there's a nice rocky climb, followed by an equally nice descent. This is where the action is. Beyond that, a couple more quick dips and lots more fast single-track bring you to the remains of an old gristmill, where you'll hang another right to reconnect with the beginning. Get a few laps in, and a dip in one of the park's many swimming spots will feel that much better.

Pace Bend Park

Location: Austin.

Distance: 4 miles.

Time: 30 minutes.

Tread: Mix of singletrack and doubletrack.

Aerobic level: Easy.

Technical difficulty: 2.

Highlights: Easy access to Lake Travis, low visitation in the off months, and no leash regulations make this one of the few great places where you can (legally) spend a day on your bike with your hound in hot pursuit. Plenty of space for camping and swimming means you can spend a nice couple of days here.

Land status: Travis County Park.

Maps: Free map at park headquarters; USGS Pace Bend.

Access: Take TX 71 west from Austin. About 15 miles past RR 620, turn right at RR 2322. Take this about 4 miles to the park entrance. There's a fee of $5.00 per vehicle for day use. Follow the park road around to the opposite side of the peninsula from the entrance; park in the area across from the road to Kate's Cove.

Notes on the trail: Though it's not really much of a mountain biking destination, Pace Bend Park does have its virtues. Chief among these, aside from the cliff jumping that attracts gaggles of inebriated young men to tempt height—and fate—all summer long, is the lack of pet leash regulations. This is one of the few (or only?) places in the state of Texas to take your hound out on a ride and not worry about getting glares from other trail users or lectures and fines from rangers.

The trail is made more for a leisurely stroll afoot than it is for tearing about on two knobby tires, but some speedy downhills and nice views make it worthwhile. And that look of slobbering, unbridled joy in your dog's big brown eyes as he tries to stick to your back wheel will make it worth all the effort.

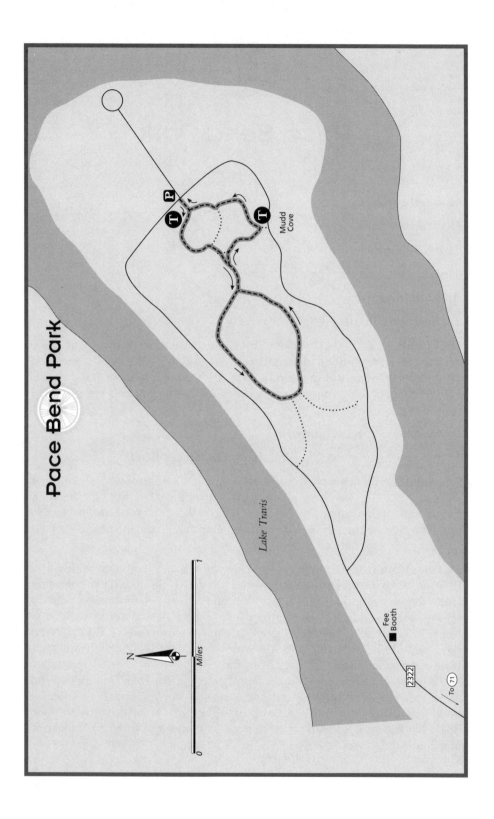

Pace Bend Park

N

0 Miles 1

Lake Travis

Mudd Cove

T P
T

Fee Booth

2322

To 71

This park has gone to the dogs—and thank goodness for that! It's a rare place that lets your hounds chase your bike untethered. Here's Gus and Henry romping in Lake Travis.

The Ride

There are two access points from the road: one on the eastern edge, leading off from the road past a low metal gate across from the rest rooms by Mudd Cove, and the one documented here, from the far end of the park. The trail is not marked in any particular direction or with any consistency—indeed, it's hardly marked at all. I tackled it in roughly counterclockwise fashion, staying to the right at the major junctions (except for the one leading out to the road by Mudd Cove) and retracing the missed inner portion of the loop, as well as some paths not on the park map, after arriving back at the first loop. This way is neither worse nor better than any other way.

The trail is mostly pebble-strewn hardpack or soft brown dirt dotted with baby-head rocks, partially shaded by thick juniper and mesquite, though much of it is exposed. There are some outstanding views of Lake Travis (and of the rampant development along its shores) from the upper reaches of the southernmost loop.

Some of the trail gets narrow and very rocky, good for hiking but not for biking unless you're the trials type. The lack of markers can also make it a bit tough to find your way around, but being that the trail is surrounded by a paved road, which is surrounded by water, you can't get lost for long. Just wander where you will—heck, if you brought the dog, let him (or her) do the leading for a change. And keep in mind that you're likely not the only one who appreciates the leash-free zone, so watch out for other dogs suddenly appearing on the path.

Muleshoe Recreation Area

Location: Austin.

Distance: 7-mile loop.

Time: 45 minutes.

Tread: Singletrack.

Aerobic level: Moderate.

Technical difficulty: 3.

Highlights: A fun, well-planned, beautiful loop of singletrack with only moderate traffic, Muleshoe Recreation Area is a great place for bikers looking for a place to either crank out a few quick laps or spend a whole weekend. Situated just outside Austin's city limits, the trail traverses the tree-covered hills along the shore of Lake Travis, passing plentiful camping facilities and enough shoreline for a refreshing postride dip.

Land status: LCRA recreation area.

Maps: Free map at park headquarters; USGS Pace Bend.

Access: Take Texas Highway 71 west from Austin to County Road 404 (called PALEFACE RANCH ROAD on a small street sign at the turnoff), and turn right. Follow this for about 5 miles, and then turn right at CR 414. After about 3 miles the road leads right into the Muleshoe Recreation Area. There's a parking area just behind the fee box and kiosk; pay your $5.00 and park. The trail crosses the road just beyond this parking area. Facing the trail from here, start out to the left—the trail is marked one-way.

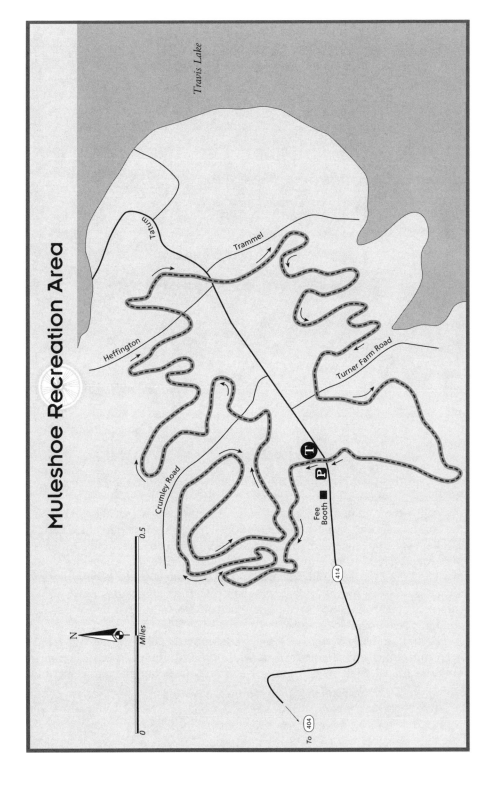

Muleshoe Recreation Area

Travis Lake

Tatum

Trammel

Heffington

Turner Farm Road

Crumley Road

Fee
Booth

P

T

414

To 404

N

Miles

0   0.5

The Muleshoe Trail is the best thing to happen to mountain biking in Austin in a long time. This is one of those trails that'll give back as much as you put into it—and here's John giving it his all.

Notes on the trail: The folks in the local cycling group, the Austin Ridge Riders, are the ones to thank for making this trail happen. Working with the LCRA they helped design and build the singletrack that loops around the serene acres of Muleshoe Recreation Area. It's a wonderful ride that can be a workout for the expert or a smooth outing for the novice. I come here for weekend rides with my beginner wife and for training rides with my hardcore brother, and the trail taken at both speeds never fails to please. And even on the rare days when the parking area has a bunch of cars in it, the trail is so spread out that you won't see too many people once you're riding.

The trail is marked very well and runs one-way, so obey the signs and keep things moving smoothly. And while the trail doesn't pose too many tough technical challenges, there are a few rocky spots that can send you sprawling if you doze off.

The Ride

0.0 Trailhead, behind entry station.

0.3 After winding through an open field, the trail dips into the trees. Loose black dirt and rock ledges going downward start you off, leading to a quick climb.

0.7 A set of switchbacks heading down offers the first opportunity to gain some speed—but definitely not the last.

1.5 The first uphill grunt of the ride, though it's a relatively mild one. There are some rocks to hop up at the top before the path flattens out again. Here, as almost everywhere on this trail, momentum goes a long way. Keep those feet turning.

2.2 The trail winds back and forth on itself before launching you into a series of quick downhills.

2.6 Crossing Crumley Road brings you to a short climb, which then brings you to a long downhill with a treacherously soft corner at the end. Many of the descents have these powdery sharp turns waiting at the bottom, so beware.

3.8 Another mile of exceedingly pleasant singletrack brings you to the second road crossing, here Heffington Road, which you'll hit on a downhill and continue to drop on the other side. The road feints to doubletrack here briefly, but then turns right back to single-track—good spot for a passing move! Just beyond this there's an open area with a fire pit near an inlet of Lake Travis. Great spot.

4.1 The trail crosses the main road just past the Heffington intersection.

4.8 Nice climb for 0.1 mile, then some more smooth, fast singletrack.

5.2 Head across Turner Farm Road here after running adjacent to the road for just a bit. There's not much auto traffic out here most days, but still, as your mother always told you, look both ways before you cross. If you're driving, be especially careful near the crossings.

5.9 A nice climb brings you to a high point in the park, where you're afforded a pretty nice view of your surroundings.

6.8 Back at the trailhead.

Rocky Hill Ranch

Location: Smithville.

Distance: 14 miles, with opportunity for more.

Time: 2 hours.

Tread: Mostly singletrack, with some short stretches on fire roads.

Aerobic level: Moderate to strenuous.

Technical difficulty: 3 to 4.

Highlights: The ultimate mountain bike ranch. Between the camping, the saloon, and the huge network of trails, this place has it all. Once past the lung-busting stretch of hills at the beginning, the trails are mostly smooth and fast. Some stretches offer roller coaster–like speed and turns, and the one-way riding lets you make the best of them.

Land status: Privately owned; fees required to ride and/or camp.

Maps: Free map with registration; USGS Smithville.

Access: From Bastrop, take U.S. 71 east to the first Smithville exit, FM 153. Turn left under the highway, and take FM 153 about 2.5 miles to the ranch's entrance on the left, marked by an old rusty bike swinging from the sign. From the parking area by the saloon, it's an easy ride down the gravel road to the trailhead.

Notes on the trail: Rocky Hill Ranch is a Central Texas biker's paradise. It's on private land, and most trails run one-way, so traffic is minimal. And although the first stretch of trail—the ominously named Fat Chuck's Demise—is a grueling series of hills covered with loose gravel, the trail network here is one of the most user-friendly configurations you'll find. The trails are all well marked, and each section can be accessed from a fire road that circles the ranch and from power line and pipeline clearings. Once the ride is over, there are bike wash facilities as well as a saloon with a great front porch, huge hamburgers, and ice-cold beer.

The beginning of this trail is difficult—but don't be discouraged. Once you manage to pedal (or walk) your way past Fat Chuck's, the terrain evens out and the ride becomes much more pleasurable. Try to think of it as a warm-up. A hefty chunk of Fat Chuck's is bypassed by taking Grey's

Rocky Hill Ranch

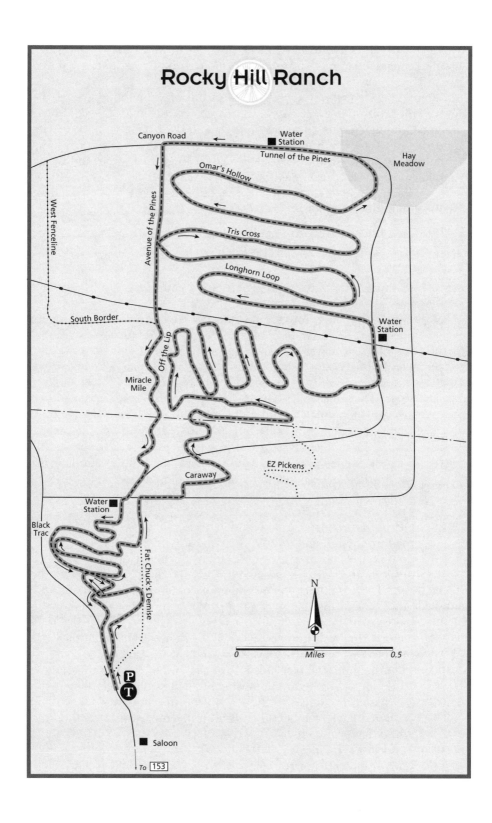

Way, a relatively smooth and rolling segment of singletrack that winds uphill through cedar, oak and prickly pear, and the Drop Zone, a bobsled run of banked turns and deep ravines.

Camping is a good way to get the most out of your time here, as the Rocky Hill trails offer great opportunities for night riding. The sight lines are good, the dangerous obstacles are few, and the course is marked with reflective foil. The ranch hosts a number of NORBA-sponsored races and an annual twenty-four-hour race. For a short time every year, the Excalibur Renaissance Fair occupies the lower reaches of the ranch (riding is still allowed), while on a normal weekend you might find a band or karaoke night at the saloon.

The Ride

0.0 Trailhead (ALL BIKES sign). There are a couple easy hills right off the bat.

0.4 The Drop Zone. You should have to wear a protective harness through this system of chutes and high-banked turns.

0.8 Ike's Peak is an extremely steep hill. Get up there!

1.0 The last segment of Fat Chuck's Demise is a nasty, loose, rocky climb.

1.1 Veer right along the plastic fence at the first water station, then take an immediate left at Caraway. This feeds into EZ Pickens, which is more of the same fast, hard-packed twisty singletrack.

2.2 Off the Lip is one of the finest pieces of singletrack in the state—a riotous series of whoop-de-dos where quick little climbs bring you to short, steep downhills that then launch you and your bike along a smooth and fast stretch of straightaway, over and over again.

3.6 Off the Lip ends at a wide gravel road. Turn left and follow the road up the hill and around the bend to Longhorn Loop.

3.8 Longhorn Loop and a water station. Turn left. This singletrack dives in and out of a creekbed again and again. A turnoff at the end of this trail lets you cut this ride to a 6-mile loop.

4.8 Tris Cross keeps things moving fast, adding a few nice climbs to the mix.

7.8 Omar's Hollow. This can get wet if it's rained lately, but otherwise this is a fast trek through the lowlands of the ranch.

9.0 In springtime, the hay meadow at the end of the Omar's Hollow Trail features some of the most spectacular wildflower viewing in the state. The field stretches far to the tree line in a surreal and colorized haze of bluebonnets and other red, purple, yellow, and white flowers.

9.3 Tunnel of the Pines.

9.6 Canyon Road water station.

9.9	Avenue of the Pines. It's long and not so exciting out here. Keep pedaling.
11.0	South Border. Curve left.
11.3	Miracle Mile brings you back into the trees for a fun run on a slight downhill.
12.1	This is the water station you passed after coming off Fat Chuck's.
12.3	Black Trac is the grand finale of the course. Tight turns, steep drops, and a couple killer climbs attempt to finish you off. If they don't, The Wall will. It's a hair-whitening drop and a huge climb straight up. If your nerve will get you down, your momentum will carry you back up. From here, follow the trail as it winds back through the last of the forested acres before spitting you out along the ranch road on the way to the trailhead.
13.9	Back at the start.

Central Texas
Honorable Mentions

Ⓒ Cameron Park

Location: Waco.

Distance: 8 miles.

Time: 1.5 hours.

Tread: Mostly singletrack with some doubletrack.

Aerobic level: Strenuous.

Technical difficulty: 4.

Highlights: Tons of wonderful singletrack, including some challenging climbs and one of the sweetest downhill bombs in Texas, make this city park on the banks of the Brazos a great biking destination.

Land status: City Park.

Maps: A crude map is available from Outback Bikes in Waco; USGS Waco West.

Access: Take I–35 to Waco; get off on exit 334 to South Seventeenth Street and head west. Keep to the road when it jogs left at Bosque, and turn right at North Eighteenth Street. Go 1.5 miles and stay to the left when the road becomes North Nineteenth Street. After another 0.5 mile, turn right at Park Lake Drive and go into the park to the Lover's Leap parking lot. On your bike, follow the road back out of the parking lot and turn into the field on your right through the opening in the curb. The singletrack dips down into the trees at the far end of the field, 0.1 mile away from the car.

Notes on the trail: The trails at Cameron Park are numerous and interlaced, so odds are that you'll invent a loop of your own after riding here a couple times. The trails cover some good-sized hills and bluffs that make for more climbing than you probably thought you'd find in Waco. Be careful out there, though, and keep your eyes on the turf; there's tons of broken glass whenever the trail comes near any of the many parking lots or easily accessible areas.

The ride: Unless the course has been recently marked for a race, trying to follow written directions for a loop on your first trip to Cameron Park would soon prove maddening. The place is a veritable maze of singletrack with too many intersections to be accounted for. Besides, if you've got your nose in a guidebook trying to figure out where to turn right and which way is northeast, you'll be missing out on all the fun. My advice, as it often is, is to follow someone who knows. In lieu of local assistance, try to stick to the trails that look as though they've seen recent traffic. And don't stay low—if you shy away from the long climbs, you'll be missing out on some heart-racing downhills. And people think Waco is flat . . .

Many of the trails have been named and marked with ski-rating symbols, which will help if you feel you're going in circles. When the black diamonds break away from the blue squares, you can bet the diamonds involve some hairy inclines. They usually hook back up with the easier trail within a mile, so you've got lots of choices. Gauge your lungs, your legs, and your balance—then take the tough route! Still, markers or not, you *will* find yourself going in circles. But getting lost out here is no big deal, as you're wedged in between some residential developments and the southern shore of the Brazos River. So don't worry. Just ride.

These are serious trails, by the way. Quad-burning climbs and eye-watering downhills are studded with roots and stumps and rocks, so blind speed is not the best policy out here. Respect the terrain, and you'll have a better ride than you ever thought possible in this part of the state. I mean it, this place is amazing. Dark, rich soil; near-constant tree cover; and the beautiful Brazos River combine with miles and miles of technically challenging singletrack for one of the best mountain biking parks in Texas. Again, watch for broken glass, especially when the trail nears a road or a parking lot.

D Shoal Creek Greenbelt

Location: Austin.

Distance: 4 miles one-way.

Time: 0.5 hour one-way.

Tread: Mix of hike and bike, singletrack, and street.

Aerobic level: Easy.

Technical difficulty: 1.

Highlights: An effective way to get across town as well as a fun ride in and of itself, the Shoal Creek Greenbelt provides bikers with access to the Town Lake Hike and Bike, Duncan Park, and Pease Park as it runs straight up through a main corridor of the city, sheltered by trees and insulated from auto traffic most of the way.

Land status: City Park.

Maps: Map available on-line at www.txinfo.com; USGS Austin East.

Access: The easiest access point is from Pease Park, at about the center of the trail. Exit I–35 at Thirty-eighth Street and go west to Lamar. Turn left and go south to Twenty-fourth Street. Turn right, and then take your first left after crossing Shoal Creek. There are a few parking areas along this road behind Pease Park. You can also access this path and any number of points along its route, generally tracing the west side of Lamar Boulevard from Lake Austin up to Thirty-eighth Street.

Notes on the trail: Though not a full-on mountain bike ride, this trail is worthy of mention because some parts of it are fun dirt riding, and it allows you to tool around the city on fat tires without resorting to streets and the traffic and traffic lights that go along with them.

The ride: Between the Town Lake Trail and about Sixth Street, this isn't the easiest trail to navigate. But with a bit of urban exploration, you can follow unknown and/or abandoned paths below the street's surface along usually dry Shoal Creek and emerge just south of Sixth and Lamar. From there the going is a bit easier, especially from Fifteenth Street north through Pease Park. The trail splits and runs on both sides of the creek through the park. There's a playground, a killer disc golf course, and more than a few acres of space perfect for plain old hanging out. North of Twenty-ninth Street the trail gets a bit away from the creek, but it's still easy to follow and doesn't peter out until north of Thirty-eighth at Shoal Creek Boulevard. (Shoal Creek Boulevard has a great bike lane, too, if you need to keep heading north.)

Bluff Creek Ranch

Location: Warda.

Distance: 9.3-mile loop.

Time: 1.5 hours.

Tread: Mostly singletrack.

Aerobic level: Moderate.

Technical difficulty: 3.

Highlights: A well-marked one-way intermediate ride through a piney forest with a few challenging downhills and climbs on the bluff (as well as bypass routes) and plenty of twisty-turny singletrack. Hospitable to riders of all levels, Bluff Creek Ranch is one of the most bike-friendly places you'll ever visit.

Land status: Privately owned. At the time of writing, there was a possibility that Bluff Creek Ranch was being sold. So the ranch's future as a MTB destination is in doubt. Call an Austin bike shop to check on the status before heading out.

Maps: Free map at ranch house; USGS Warda.

Access: Take U.S. 77 south from Giddings about 10 miles to Warda, and turn off on Owl Creek Road, which is across the street just before the Warda Store (or about 4.8 miles north from FM 153 coming from the other direction). The ranch entrance is marked by a sign on the left side, 0.5 mile down Owl Creek Road. Follow the gravel road through the touch-fence around the bend to the left to the first building on the right for registration. The trailhead is well marked, at a cattleguard along the road in.

Notes on the trail: The hospitality of the Nolan family, owners and operators of Bluff Creek Ranch, is apparent from the moment you enter their property. Longhorn cattle, Arabian horses, and mountain bikers are the inhabitants of this 200-acre Central Texas ranch, and all are well taken care of. Riders register right in the Nolans' living room, and you can always count on an update on trail conditions before you start out. There are plenty of camping spaces available around a sizable water tank, and showers and rest rooms are also available to day users.

The ride is not a difficult one, but even though kids and beginners can be comfortable here, the trail does offer enough challenging terrain to get a good sweat out of any level rider. The trail moves one-way; keep the blue ribbons to your right. Smooth and fast singletrack crosses and recrosses a creekbed and bluff, and in addition to the cedars and oaks that are abundant in this region, the trails at Bluff Creek are largely covered by a lush canopy of loblolly pines—part of the Lost Pines region of Central Texas.

The course is tight and winding from the get-go, but once accustomed to the surface, you can maintain good speed through the corners. Many quick downhills shoot you through a shallow creekbed, and the climbs leading out of them usually take a sharp turn along the creek.

The ride: The first section of trail, called 100 Aker Woods, winds back and forth, getting the most trail out of every acre. The surface is mostly hardpack covered with pine needles, though some stretches of ashy ground, especially through corners, can threaten your balance. It's common to cross paths with some of the longhorn cattle that graze the ranch, especially in the Cattle Rest section, but for the most part they stay clear of the trail. (If they're in your way, make noise and wave your arms, and the cattle will move. Just don't get into a staring contest with a bull—trust me on this one.) A pipeline, power lines, and two roads offer through-ways that cross the trails at several points—in case you want an early escape from the 100 Aker Woods or to backtrack to repeat a section. The only difficult section of trail here, marked OH S_IT!, offers a long downhill punctuated with rises that could catch you unawares if you're not paying attention. But don't brake too much—quite a long climb starts immediately at the bottom.

After a few more miles of tight, fast singletrack, you'll cross the cattleguard to leave this section (be careful—the cattleguard ramps are fairly steep); a long narrow trail leads you along the fenceline toward the back stretch of the ranch. This is where the action is. Gas Pass starts it off—an extremely steep, paved downhill that turns severely to the right as soon as you hit the bottom. Be very careful here, and note that there is a bypass route for this section. You'll circle a broad meadow after this descent, and then you're climbing The Pass, the longest climb of the trail. Then, right away, comes Mule Trace, a steep, log-stepped drop off the bluff that's railed in by bales of hay (just in case you get ahead of yourself). Another climb brings you out of Henry Ford to Paydirt Bridge, then its up, up, up (with the assistance of some half-buried chain-link fence for traction, which works surprisingly well) until you reach ground zero. A quick zip through the aptly named Rollar Coasters and around the camp area, and you're back at the barn where you started. No doubt you'll want another lap.

The showers in the barn are free, the tank is usually good for a quick swim, and the Nolans provide free firewood to be shared among the campers as well as a number of permanent grills. Bluff Creek Ranch is as comfortable a place to ride as any in the state, and camping is a great way to get full use of a day out here. If the ranch ends up being closed to bikers, it'll be a tragic loss.

 F McAllister Park

Location: San Antonio.

Distance: 12 miles.

Time: 1.5 hours.

Tread: Mostly singletrack, some doubletrack, some park road.

Aerobic level: Moderate.

Technical difficulty: 3.

Highlights: A great big park in the midst of a great big city, McAllister Park offers a great mix of easy and intense riding that's usually surprisingly isolated from the park's busier areas.

Land status: City Park.

Maps: On-line map available at the South Texas Off Road Mountain Bike (STORM) home page: www.storm-web.org; USGS Longhorn.

Bob and Chris show us out-of-towners how it's done at McAllister Park. If you see these guys on the trail, follow them (if you can keep up). They know this place better than anyone.

126

Access: From San Antonio, take U.S. 281 north toward Johnson City to the Bitters exit. Exit and turn right. When the road splits, stay left on Starcrest. Turn left again on Jones-Maltberger. The park entrance is on the right after the police station. After entering the park, go straight at the T and park near the back of the park by Pavilion #3. The trail crosses the park road, so double back on your bike toward the entrance and turn left onto the trail (right, if you're facing the way you came in).

Notes on the trail: As with most trails in the San Antonio area, development has taken a heavy toll on the trails at McAllister Park. Where once they sprawled for miles in many directions, now they're cut off and subdivided into shorter sections in each of the trail system's four main quadrants.

There are miles and miles of trail throughout McAllister Park, but only familiarity and many hours of exploration can make you feel like you know where you're going here. Lack of any comprehensive map, trail markings, or even an uninterrupted loop can make it a real challenge to piece together a ride if you're not familiar with the trails. Once again, my advice is to follow a local. In lieu of that assistance, just keep at it. Despite the development, there are still many miles of fantastic singletrack out here.

Ⓖ Government Canyon State Park

Location: San Antonio.

Distance: 17-mile loop.

Time: Unknown.

Tread: Mostly singletrack, some doubletrack.

Aerobic level: Unknown.

Technical difficulty: Unknown.

Highlights: A brand-new trail such as this is a heralded event in a city whose trails are disappearing far too quickly. With the development at 700 Acres and even McAllister Park putting a damper on San Antonio off-road opportunities, the grand opening of the new Government Canyon State Park is just what the doctor ordered.

Land status: State Park, opening sometime in 2002.

Maps: Unknown.

Access: Take Loop 1604 to FM 471 (Culebra Road) and go west. After 3.5 miles turn right on Galm Road and go north 1.6 miles. There's a gate with a sign on the left.

Notes on the trail: At the time of this writing, these trails were not yet officially opened. The park was slated for a grand opening at the end of

2001 or the beginning of 2002, but these things can get delayed. Keep an eye on the Texas Parks and Wildlife Department Web site (www.state.tx.us/park/parks.htm) for further information.

The ride: The park lies on the Balcones Escarpment, which means rocky terrain covered in cedar, live oak, and cottonwood—and an abundance of canyons.

Panhandle

Folks from the Panhandle, that squared-off portion of the state that juts northward between Oklahoma and New Mexico, will tell you that the wind can drive you crazy—literally insane. Believe it. The endless expanses of flat, flat ground broken only by low shrubby vegetation and towns that stand defiant in the face of the elements are most definitely, as legendary Lubbock native Butch Hancock sings it, the Wind's Dominion. It blows and it blows and it blows. Winter brings freezing temperatures and often a good amount of snowfall; summer turns the hard-baked terrain into a cast-iron frying pan every day. This is the Llano Estacado, and it's rough country.

But leave the freeways, get away from the sprawling towns, look a little harder, and you'll come across great canyons that carve their way across the land like subterranean oases, hosting flowing waterways and the vegetation and animal life that accompany them. And they're beautiful. Rock blazes red and orange, standing layer upon layer in weird and haunting formations. The constant weathering of the sedimentary rock makes for an eerie landscape in these canyon bottoms. It also makes for fast, smooth trails. The rides up here are few and far between, but they're most definitely worth the effort.

Where the Capitol Peak Trail is a mini-Moab, fast and smooth along shocking red rock and dirt, the Quitaque Canyon Rails to Trails is a long meander across miles and miles of the Panhandle plains. Both are beautiful rides—as are their counterparts over in Copper Breaks and Caprock Canyon State Parks—and both are approachable by riders of any level, as the others are not. Up here, you have to know your limits and be prepared for the worst. Weather changes quickly and ferociously, and miles from nowhere with no shade or shelter is not the place to be when a big storm breaks.

Scary stuff aside, there's some great riding to do up here. Come in spring or fall, and you'll have an experience you won't soon forget.

Quitaque Canyon/Los Lingos Rails to Trails

Location: From South Plains to Estilline, in the eastern portion of the Panhandle.

Distance: 25 miles as documented here; 65 miles total.

Time: 2.5 hours for the 25-mile section.

Tread: Smooth, crushed limestone on a converted railroad bed.

Aerobic level: Moderate.

Technical difficulty: 1.

Highlights: This rail trail is a fairly easy way to cover a lot of ground and see miles of stunning caprock scenery. Unlike the trails in Caprock Canyons State Park, the lack of any technical challenges out here means you can devote most of your attention to your surroundings. And you will be constantly amazed. This is the ranching country of legend, and you can practically see the cowboys leading the herd through the canyon bottoms, kicking up giant clouds of red dust along the way.

Land status: Railroad easement maintained and managed by TPWD.

Maps: Free map at park headquarters; USGS Lake Theo, Turkey.

Access: From Plainview, just east of I–27 south of Amarillo, take U.S. 70 east to FM 400 and turn left. About 1 mile later, turn right on FM 2286 and follow this for 15 miles. At FM 378 you have to jog north about 1 mile, then reconnect with FM 2286 and turn right, toward South Plains. Pass over County Road 207, and 2 miles later turn left on Country Road 189. Go north 0.9 mile and park by the trailhead on the right. The trail heads out to the east past the gate.

Notes on the trail: The mountains of West Texas are the grandest monuments, and the Hill Country in the center of the state is home to the state's most picturesque and pastoral settings. But the caprock area, here in the Panhandle, offers the most striking scenery in the Lone Star State. The floor of the high plains opens up to expose red rock as vivid as the best of sunsets and canyon walls as steep and striated—if not as big—as that

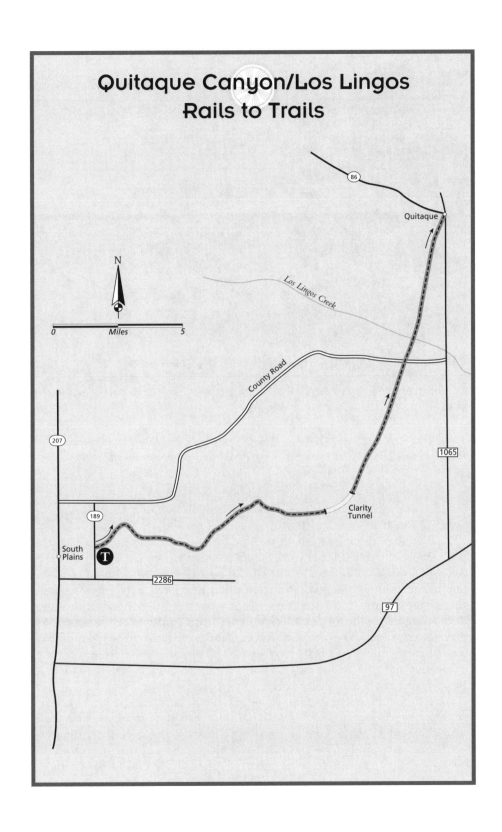

Quitaque Canyon/Los Lingos
Rails to Trails

N

0   Miles   5

86

Quitaque

Los Lingos Creek

County Road

207

1065

189

Clarity
Tunnel

South
Plains

T

2286

97

The old railroad bed of the Quitaque Canyon Rails to Trails is the perfect surface for a long day of spinning and sight-seeing. The red rock and canyons along the way are spectacular.

grander canyon out in Arizona. This is canyon country, Wile E. Coyote land. You've just got to see it.

And what better way to see it than on a bike? I haven't done this whole trail—in its entirety it leads from South Plains a whopping 65 miles to the town of Estilline. I've been told that the best part is the section between South Plains and Quitaque, and from what I saw out here I don't doubt that's true. If you've got the time, the support, and the energy, I imagine that riding this trail from end to end would be a gratifying experience. As it was, I had help, and the trail from near South Plains to Quitaque was amazing enough. Reportedly you can purchase a shuttle from Caprock Canyons State Park to the South Plains Trailhead, which would allow you to cover the route I describe here on a one-way outing.

You probably won't see much wildlife out here except for the tiny, scampering variety and the occasional deer, but the landscape and rock formations more than make up for the feeling of being the only living critter for miles around. The grade is exceedingly easy, probably around an even 1 percent the whole way, downhill from either end to the halfway point at Clarity Tunnel, so speed is a definite possibility. It's time to put that big ring to some use!

The Ride

Don't let the first mile from the trailhead fool you. Though it starts out flat and fairly uninteresting, just after the 1-mile mark the scenery takes a turn for the better, turning suddenly from dry farmland to red-rock canyon. As you descend gently into low canyon grooves, passing dark rock walls and traversing a few wooden bridges, you'll likely pass large piles of railroad ties left at the side of the trail. They had to put them somewhere after pulling them all up, right?

At nearly the halfway point, about the 12-mile mark, you'll hit the Clarity Tunnel, which until about twenty-five years ago was the last operating railroad tunnel in the state of Texas. It's a fairly quick trip through the tunnel, but definitely an interesting one. The ceiling will likely be lined with loads of Mexican freetail bats, and the floor will definitely be nearly covered with guano. Be careful, and follow the line cleared through the center—the powder from that stuff can be slippery.

Shortly after the tunnel the trail begins a gradual upward grade toward Monk's Crossing at a county road near Los Lingos Creek. If the wind isn't in your face, it's fairly easy going. If it is, bear down and trudge on. You'll pass over Los Lingos Creek and another county road before reaching Quitaque, where you'll pick up your ride, retreat to the state park to the west along TX 86, or turn around for the return trip. As always for a trail of this length, bring plenty of water and a little something to eat, because this can be a long day in the saddle.

Caprock Canyon Trail

Location: Caprock Canyons State Park, Quitaque.

Distance: 5.5-mile loop.

Time: 1 hour.

Tread: Mostly doubletrack, some singletrack.

Aerobic level: Moderate.

Technical difficulty: 3.

Highlights: Silence, isolation, and tremendous views of the dramatic caprock scenery are reasons enough to make your way out to Quitaque and take a spin on the bike. In addition to the Quitaque Canyon Rails to Trails, there are two separate loops in Caprock Canyons State Park that deserve your attention; both offer awesome vistas and a few technical challenges.

Land status: State Park.

Maps: Free map at park headquarters; USGS Lake Theo and Turkey.

Access: From I–27 south of Amarillo, take TX 86 east toward Quitaque. Turn north on FM 1065 and go about 4 miles to the park entrance. After paying fees at headquarters, go back out the way you came and turn left on FM 1065. At the first dirt county road turn left and follow the road north about 2.5 miles to the trailhead at a gate on your right. Head out east from here.

Notes on the trail: In some places, this trail is not much of a trail. It's fairly easy to wander off the main path, since it's not marked the whole way around. But, much like the riding in Big Bend Ranch State Park, the reason to ride this trail is to commune with the natural surroundings, not to have an "extreme MTB" experience. Your efforts will be rewarded not only with amazing views but also with a sense of completed adventure upon arriving back at the trailhead.

But the views! Like its neighbor, Palo Duro Canyon, Caprock Canyons State Park boasts scenery so splendid as to be fairly incongruous with the part of the state it calls home. Not that plains and flatlands don't have their own kind of beauty—they do—but the dramatic shades of red and the eons

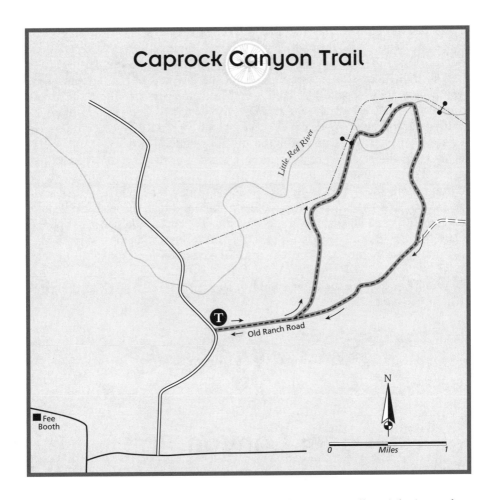

Caprock Canyon Trail

Little Red River

T
← Old Ranch Road →

Fee
Booth

N

0   Miles   1

of history laid bare in the layers of exposed canyon walls might just take your breath away.

At one time this was the only trail in Caprock Canyons State Park open to mountain bikes, but now a portion of the Canyon Trail system has been opened and even hosts a NORBA event each year, the Quitaque Quest. I haven't participated as yet, but I definitely plan to do so.

The Ride

Before you start make sure to get the combination to the entrance from headquarters. The trail starts out easy enough, as you'll follow the nice surface of Old Ranch Road out from the gate at the trailhead for a little over a mile. The trailhead is marked, as is the first split, at about 1.2 miles, where the loop departs the ranch road to your left. Beyond this point, you'll get little help from signage as you make your way down toward the

Little Red River. The way down is a steep, rocky descent with plenty of loose stuff and tricky drops to get you white-knuckled and sweaty. Relax, stick to your lines, and work your way carefully down to the bottom.

The trail follows a fenceline for about the last half of the descent, and you'll pass another gate just before you hit the river—or where the river would be if it weren't always dry. Down by the riverbed, watch for rock cairns and follow the path north and east as it traces the riverbed 0.5 mile or so. Keep your eyes open for the partially hidden dirt road that leads away from the riverbed for the climb back out of the canyon. It took me a bit of wandering to find it. When you do find it, you'll begin a tough climb up the steep canyon walls over loose, rocky terrain. This is granny-gear stuff, so take your time, get your rhythm, and turn those cranks again and again. If you do stop along the way, it's OK. You *should* pause to appreciate the view of the canyon floor behind you. But don't stop for too long. Keep moving; before you know it, you'll be back on top at the Old Ranch Road.

When you hit the road, turn right; it's about 1.5 miles back to the gate where you came in.

Lower Canyon Trail

Location: Caprock Canyons State Park, Quitaque.

Distance: 6.5-mile loop.

Time: 1.5 hours.

Tread: Mix of singletrack and doubletrack.

Aerobic level: Moderate to strenuous.

Technical difficulty: 3.

Highlights: The rugged canyons of the High Plains Caprock make for a dramatic transition between the high plains of the Panhandle and the lower plains to the east. Red sandstone, shale, and gypsum stripe the canyon walls in precise striations; sparse mesquite and juniper add their dusty greens and browns to enhance the shocking color of the land from which they grow. Yep, it's purty out there.

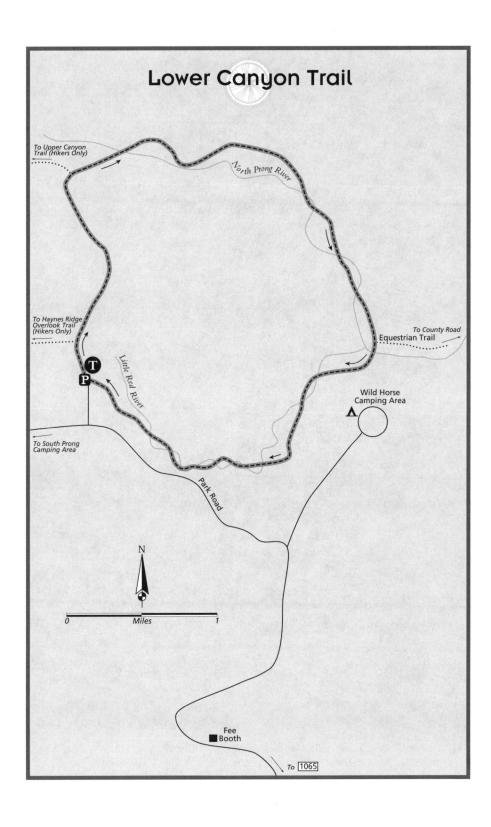

Lower Canyon Trail

To Upper Canyon
Trail (Hikers Only)

North Prong River

To Haynes Ridge
Overlook Trail
(Hikers Only)

To County Road

Equestrian Trail

T

P

Little Red River

Wild Horse
Camping Area

To South Prong
Camping Area

Park Road

N

0   Miles   1

Fee
Booth

To 1065

The Lower Canyon Trail offers stunning canyon panoramas along the way. The riding here is a blast, but make sure you get off the bike and check out some of the Upper Canyon's scenic overlooks.

Land status: State Park.

Maps: Free map at park headquarters; USGS Lake Theo.

Access: From I–27 south of Amarillo, take TX 86 east toward Quitaque. Turn north on FM 1065 and go about 4 miles to the park entrance. Past headquarters, follow the park road as it bends right past the Honea Flat camping area. Follow the road all the way to the parking area for the Lower Canyon Trail. The trail heads out north from here.

Notes on the trail: The trail documented here is one-half of the whole canyon trail complex that links the North Prong and South Prong Rivers with Haynes Ridge in the northwest corner of the park. It's probably the most scenic and accessible part of the park, and therefore sees the most traffic, which still isn't so very heavy. But remember, this is a multiuse trail, which means bikers yield to hikers and equestrians. Be polite; there's plenty of room in this canyon for everyone.

If you don't stick a camera in your pocket for this ride, you'll wish you had. The deep reds and oranges of the canyon walls and the red dirt under-wheel make for dramatic backdrops, and a number of points along the way seem prime spots for designated scenic overlooks.

The Lower Canyon Trail is used for the Quitaque Quest, a NORBA-sanctioned race that takes place in the park every year. It's a fairly grueling route at race pace, so if your goal is to compete here, you'll definitely want to spend a weekend prior to the race getting familiar with the trail.

The Ride

From the parking area, the trail heads out to the north (left) over some rolling hills, which makes for a good warm-up. If you plan on hitting the trail hard, you might want to take a bit of a spin on the park road first to get those legs warm, as it's not too long before you hit some fairly strenuous climbing.

After a mere half mile or so, you'll start climbing. It's all singletrack here, but the going can be fairly loose and rocky and the inclines pretty steep at times. At about the 1-mile mark, there's a narrow dirt path leading off to the left. This is the Haynes Ridge Overlook Trail—for foot traffic only. A short way up this trail, past a set of switchbacks, is a scenic overlook point whose view of the canyon could make a grown man weep. It's well worth the time to get back out here and tackle these trails on foot, but save that for another day and keep riding.

Past this turnoff you'll continue to climb a little before turning downward to make the descent to the North Prong River. This is a drop of about 0.5 mile, most of it reasonable and a few spots fairly treacherous. At 1.6 miles or so, hit a trail junction and turn right. There are no bikes allowed to the left, which is the Upper Canyon Trail, part of the hiking loop that includes the Haynes Ridge Trail.

Follow the right-hand trail through the lower reaches, crossing the river at one point, which is not a problem. The trail bends to the east and reconnects with the riverbed, following it more than 2 miles until it hits a junction with an equestrian trail near the Wild Horse camping area. The going here can be pretty rough and not so clear at times, but for the most part the trail is well defined; you may luck out and get to follow the race markers if the race has been run recently. At the next junction, keep to the right, leaving the bed of the North Prong and following the Little Red River back to the west. A combination of speedy singletrack and mushy, rocky riverbed brings you 2.5 miles back to the parking area, approaching it from the south. There are some big drops and steep climbs down here, traversing banks and short cliff sides, and one in particular toward the end of the trail is worth heeding. It's very steep and the surface is not so dependable; be careful.

Copper Breaks State Park Trail

Location: Copper Breaks State Park, south of Quanah.

Distance: 9-mile loop.

Time: 2 hours.

Tread: Mostly doubletrack.

Aerobic level: Easy to moderate.

Technical difficulty: 2.

Highlights: Rugged scenery, low visitation, and a staff that's eager to help you enjoy your time in this park all combine to make riding in Copper Breaks State Park a very pleasant experience. It's not the most exciting riding in the state, but it's got its virtues—like some speedy hardpack through wide-open terrain and the fact that it's one of the few places to ride in this area. A portion of the Texas longhorn herd also resides in the park, so roll by and moo them a big hello.

Land status: State Park.

Maps: Free map at park headquarters; USGS Teacup Mountain and Margaret.

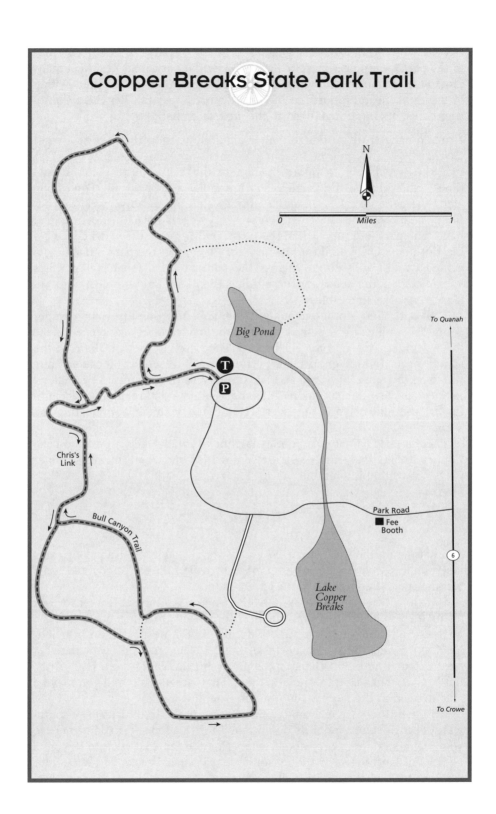

Copper Breaks State Park Trail

N

0   Miles   1

Big Pond

T

P

To Quanah

Chris's
Link

Bull Canyon Trail

Park Road

Fee
Booth

6

Lake
Copper
Breaks

To Crowe

Access: From U.S. 287 near Quanah take TX 6 south for about 13 miles to the park's entrance on your right. Follow the park road past headquarters to the Comanche camping area and continue through the intersection to the right, heading north to the parking area near the Big Pond Equestrian Area. The trail heads out to the west from here.

Notes on the trail: Although the terrain and the trails themselves are not technically challenging or treacherous, there are some places where it is exceedingly difficult to figure out where the heck you're going. Sometimes, especially on the north-to-south doubletrack of the Big Pond Loop along the park's western boundary, the trail all but disappears. Little traffic, no markers, and the even and sparsely vegetated nature of the land make one part look much like the next. You'll find yourself wandering a bit. But that's OK, you'll find it. Just carry a copy of the park's map and a compass and you'll either recross the path or hit a fence. Or perhaps you've got a better sense for these things than I do and will have no problems. Anything's possible.

That said, there's much to enjoy riding here. You won't pass many other people; most likely it'll be just you and the roadrunners, which can make for a wonderful day in and of itself. It'd be awfully hot out here in the summertime, but fall or spring is perfect for riding, when you can actually welcome the sun on your face. Flat, scrubby badlands striped by shallow ravines and low, mean-looking hills make this park threateningly beautiful; by the end of your time here, you'll find yourself appreciating the scenery.

There are also plenty of camping facilities as well as the good-sized Lake Copper Breaks for your postride cool-down swim, which makes summer visits not wholly intolerable.

The Ride

As my time on the trails involved much wandering and retracing of paths taken and missed, I will not attempt to provide mileage points and exact turning spots. I couldn't even if I wanted to.

Starting at the parking area, take the trail out to the southwest for just about 0.25 mile. At the first junction turn right, heading north along a hoof-scarred doubletrack for about a mile. At the next junction bear left, heading toward the park's northern border. The trail can be somewhat faint through here, but the going is pretty quick. There are a few cairns, but I found that I couldn't rely on them. Slow down a bit, and you may be able to keep to the path without much trouble.

After a little less than a mile in this direction, the trail turns back southward, losing even more of its definition. There's a fence off somewhere to your right, so don't worry about wandering too far. Just stick to the open patches of land between the mesquite and juniper breaks and keep your eyes out for a trail crossing east to west.

When you hit this junction, head to your right and follow the wide singletrack as it loops around back to the south. This is called Chris's Link, and it's a fairly well defined mile of singletrack that connects the Big Pond area to the Bull Canyon Trail. It's a matter of only a few minutes, more like twenty actually, to get around this loop, but it's a fun, fast ride that is easier to follow than the northern section.

The two loops of the Bull Canyon Trail add up to about 3 miles, after which you'll get back onto Chris's Link and head back northward. One mile later, back at the intersection, turn right and take the doubletrack about 0.5 mile to the junction with the spur trail to the parking area. Turn right here and you're soon back at your vehicle.

Note: Keep your eye on the sky, as the weather in this part of the state can turn on you pretty dang quick. Out here in the wide open is not a place you want to be if the clouds decide to crack. Trust me on this one.

Capitol Peak/Lighthouse Trail

Location: Palo Duro Canyon State Park, near Canyon.

Distance: 7.5 miles round-trip.

Time: 1.25 hours.

Tread: Mix of singletrack and wide single path.

Aerobic level: Moderate.

Technical difficulty: 3.

Highlights: The blank plains of the Texas Panhandle, somewhere between Lubbock and Amarillo, open suddenly into one of the most beautiful spots in the whole state. Palo Duro Canyon boasts stunning views of sheer canyon walls and red-rock formations that would seem more at home near Moab, Utah, than on the windy flatlands of far north Texas.

Land status: State Park.

Maps: Free map at park headquarters; USGS Fortress Cliffs.

Access: Take I–27 south from Amarillo to TX 217 near Canyon and go east about 8 miles to Park Road 5 at the park's entrance. Follow Park Road 5 south to the parking area for the Capitol Peak MTB Trail.

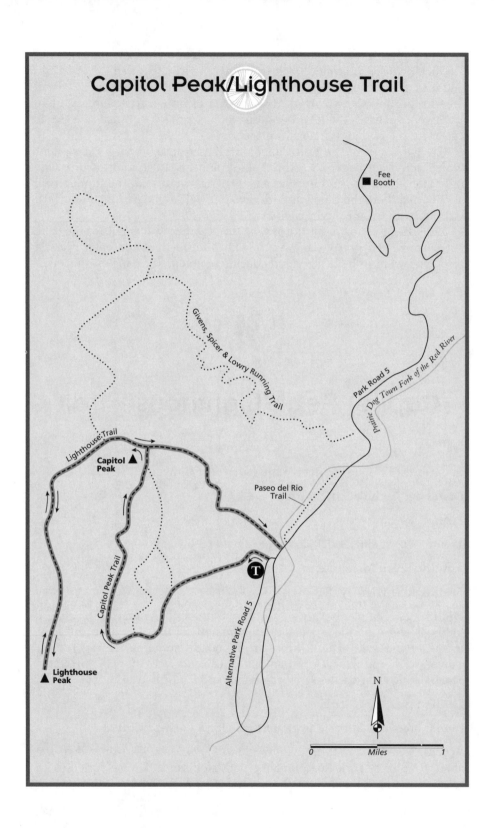

It isn't Moab, but it's close enough. Texas's own red rock is fast and fun. Here's your author doing what he loves best.

Notes on the trail: Descending the park road into Palo Duro Canyon, surrounded by vivid red rock and thick groves of mesquite, juniper, and cottonwood, you'll get the feeling that you're entering a world very much apart from the endless plains you traversed to get here. And when you put tire to trail and set out on your way to Capitol Peak, your suspicions that you hit some wrinkle in the space-time fabric and ended up on the Slickrock Trail in Moab will be all but confirmed. Though this trail may not be as epic in length, height, or difficulty as that one, there's plenty to be said for the fast and smooth singletrack that winds its way through the western portion of this gorgeous state park.

The Ride

0.0   Capitol Peak trailhead. There's a bench and a donation box next to the small roadside parking area. Heading out from here, the trail splits into a T right away. Arrows point to the right, and the trail goes up and over a little ridge.

1.0 Some ultrawindy roller coaster–style singletrack leads to the first split. I chose to tackle this section of singletrack first, hitting the longer, straighter Lighthouse Trail afterward. For that route, take a left here, sticking to the outer edge of the loop. This is red rock, fast and smooth, bordered by all manner of thorned and stickered shrub and dotted with ramps and banks enough to make a biker downright giddy.

2.0 Capitol Peak comes into view—a huge, striking formation of red claystone/sandstone and white gypsum. The views are breathtaking, so don't forget to stop and look around once in a while. There are some quick climbs and drops in this part of the trail, so keep that momentum up.

2.2 The junction of the Capitol Peak and Lighthouse Trails. You can turn back and hit the singletrack you missed on the way here, the part that heads up the middle of the two loops, and then backtrack to this point. Or take a left and head out toward Lighthouse Peak (which is the mileage marked here).

3.2 Though not as curvedly thrilling as the first stretch of singletrack, the Lighthouse Trail is a blast in its own right. Long, fast chutes of hard-packed red dirt have you sailing along among the hills and towers of rock, their history laid bare in clear layers of sediment.

3.6 The turnoff for the Givens, Spicer & Lowry Running Trail. This is a scenic and rugged 5-mile trail that, although primarily for runners and hikers, is also open to bicycles. As this trail hits the main park road just a bit north of where you parked, you might want to use it as a longer return route. (If you do, go right when you hit the park road. Or you can even skip the road almost altogether, jumping back off it at River Crossing 1 and taking the Paseo del Rio Trail parallel to the park road all the way back to Crossing 2, which is right next to the Capitol Peak parking area.)

4.6 Now you come to the base of a big set of steps that lead all the way to the top of the peak. Take some time out here before heading back the way you came.

7.0 Back where the Capitol Peak and Lighthouse Trails connect. Make sure you check out the trailside geological exhibits.

7.5 Capitol Peak trailhead.

North Texas

Though best known for the sprawling concrete metroplex of the Dallas–Fort Worth area, this part of the state boasts a surprising wealth of bike trails. Hidden green pockets around either city—small stretches near Flower Mound and Duncanville and Lewisville, among others—you'll find single-track thriving like falcons in New York City or coyotes anywhere else. It moves and adapts. It grabs hold of whatever unpaved ground it can and holds it, accommodating people and their ever-growing hunger for space while staying alive and whole.

And there are people to thank for this. Of necessity, the trails have been taken in hand by those who don't want them to disappear. The Dallas Off-Road Bicycle Association (DORBA) is perhaps the biggest player in this game, building and maintaining trails on state park land, U.S. Army Corps of Engineers land, city land, and any other land where a trail can exist. If you live in the area, join up. You'll be doing yourself a favor, and you'll meet loads of active and activist bikers to boot. Also keep in mind that most of these trails are not for bikers only. Hikers and equestrians have an interest in these patches of green space as well, and cooperation among *all* use groups is the best, indeed the only, way to keep trails open.

The landscape up here is hilly, surprisingly so. In and near the metroplex, the trails seek out topographical changes and exploit them for all they're worth—as at the area's ultimate ride, Cedar Hill State Park. Rides along Lake Grapevine are flatter but no less fun. Out away from the city, Mineral Wells is flat and long, while rides in Cleburne and Glen Rose (Dinosaur Valley State Park) feature steep climbs and long descents you'll be surprised to find. These last two trails offer some fairly treacherous technical riding as well, so be careful. They're a pretty significant change from the fun though safe and smooth rides nearer to town. In the far north, almost in Oklahoma, the Bar H Ranch is home to some of the most outrageously fun trails in the state. One big lump of a hill provides a few ridiculous climbs and a few downhills that'll have you airborne whether you want to be or not. There are miles and miles of trail here—more than are accounted for in the documented ride.

The trails near DFW see *lots* of use—I mean tons—so there are some things to remember when riding here:
- Be courteous to other trail users, of course.
- Travel lightly. Pack it in, pack it out—even the tiny foil tabs on those gel packs.
- Don't—I repeat *don't*—ride in bad weather. Places like Cedar Hill close down trails at the first hint of a mist, but some trails operate more on the honor system.
- Trash a trail and it trashes your future riding possibilities—and those of everyone else. Don't widen trails; go over that rock or through that puddle instead of skirting it.

I know, lectures are no fun. So I'm done—let's ride!

The Breaks at Bar-H Ranch

Location: St. Jo.

Distance: 8.5-mile loop as described here, though there are more than 30 miles of trail.

Time: 1 hour as described.

Tread: Mostly singletrack, some doubletrack.

Aerobic level: Strenuous.

Technical difficulty: 4.

Highlights: The ice-cream scoop of a hill that the Bar-H trails traverse is a grunt going up and a blast coming down, and there's plenty of fast singletrack in the surrounding flatlands, too. The land is used to its maximum MTB potential; the trail design is brilliant.

Land status: Privately owned; open to bikers year-round.

Maps: Map available on-line at www.barhbreaks.com; USGS St. Jo.

Access: I–35 to Gainesville, exit 498B. Take U.S. 82 west 22.5 miles to FM 2382. Turn left and follow it into St. Jo, 4 miles to the ranch entrance on the left. Register at headquarters and head for the hill. The trail as described here starts at the hill's base and goes up, following the NORBA race route.

Notes on the trail: As any mountain biker knows, life is a quest for singletrack—which ought to make Bar-H Ranch a Holy Grail of sorts. The trails total upward of 30 miles, most of it singletrack, and the ranch is open to bikers all week long, all year round. You can pitch a tent for a few bucks, too, and make a weekend out of it.

The ranch was set up for their big NORBA race the weekend I marked this route, so the loop as described here is the intermediate/expert course for that race. It totals about 8.5 miles, but don't let that keep you from exploring the rest of the ranch. There's plenty more riding out there.

For this ride, you start at the bottom of the imposing dome-shaped hill and go pretty much straight up it until you get to the top, and then you come back down. Believe me, the blazing descents are worth the grunt to

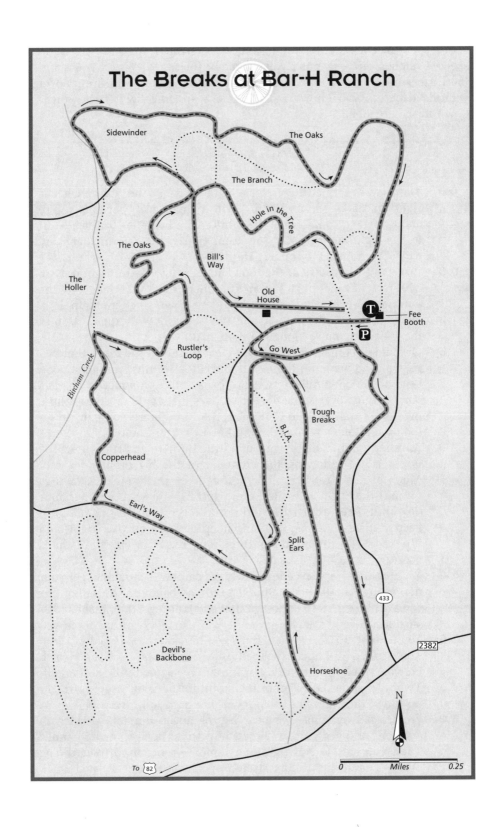

get up top. They wind down the hill in quick, steep drops and long, high-speed stretches that can push your capacity for speed. Watch yourself—there are some subtle dips and humps that can have your rear tire up over your head before you know it. There are also some tight, tricky turns down in the creekbed.

The Ride

0.0 The loop described here starts at the base of the hill and heads right up. Scoot forward and get in a small gear, because you're about to earn some sweet downhills. The beginner trail leads off to the right shortly after the climb starts; the intermediate and expert trail heads to the left and up.

0.8 Just like that, you're at the top. This is a quick gain of more than 200 feet, which puts the main ranch road that leads to the entrance just on your left. It's boulder-strewn singletrack up here.

1.0 Duck back into the woods, and then head down a quick drop in the trail and you're along the road again.

1.6 On the left is that little pink bicycle hanging on the fence that you pass on the way into the ranch. Shortly after this, you get a good taste of the downhills here. Hard-packed dirt on a nice grade gets you charging over some deceptive rises that could give you a little involuntary air. At the bottom of the hill, before you can *yahoo!* too much, take a hard right and head back up the hill.

2.0 Another tough climb evens out a little bit here and runs along the upper ridge, following the contours of the big bump of a hill. Much of this stretch is shaky, off-camber singletrack that winds up and down for a while before hitting you with another nice downhill. Keep your eyes well out ahead of you on this one; it'll keep you steady along the very steep drop-off on your right, and it'll keep you prepared for the short, really steep climb that's coming.

2.8 Yet another steep descent, slightly off-camber—enough to get your nerves in a bundle maintaining speed and balance. The end of this run will take you close to the trail's beginning through some fast singletrack full of sharp turns.

3.5 You'll come up over a small but steep hill and then drop down into The Holler, a wide creekbed that meanders back and forth between rocky terrain and singletrack for a good mile and a half.

4.5 The Sidewinder is a 15-foot highpoint in the trail; you go straight up it and then straight back down in a hard left turn.

5.0 From a narrow slickrock bed, you climb up a quick, steep path and you're out of the creekbed into some open, powdery trails. Then you start a slow, gradual hundred-foot climb toward The Oaks—a fantastic, rolling stretch of classic hardpack singletrack full of sweeping corners, whoop-de-dos, sharp rises, and long descents.

6.0 Cross a cattleguard close to the main camping area, and then head into a short climb, up and away from it. The trail above the camping area is sandy and runs along a high ridge.

6.9 Past the sign for the Horseshoe Trail, you'll encounter more short, steep stuff and lots of fast, twisty singletrack.

7.2 Jump up out of the wooded area and into a wide-open field. The trail is still singletrack here, flat and winding and very fast. This is the final area of the race course, a good spot to hit an all-out sprint for a good finish, or to cool down if you're out for fun.

8.1 The intersection for the Rustler Trail goes straight up the hill. For the race finish, keep straight, up the hill, and back to the loop in the open area near the beginning.

Lake Mineral Wells
State Trailway

Location: From Mineral Wells to Weatherford on an old railroad bed.

Distance: 20 miles one-way.

Time: 2 hours, one-way.

Tread: Old railroad bed covered in crushed limestone, like a hike and bike path.

Aerobic level: Easy.

Technical difficulty: 1.

Highlights: Rails to Trails projects are wonderful things. At their best they make good use of unused land and tie communities together with avenues other than those built for auto traffic. The Lake Mineral Wells Trailway is a great example of a good one, covering more than 20 miles of classic North Texas terrain.

Land status: State Park and trailway maintained by TPWD.

Lake Mineral Wells State Trailway

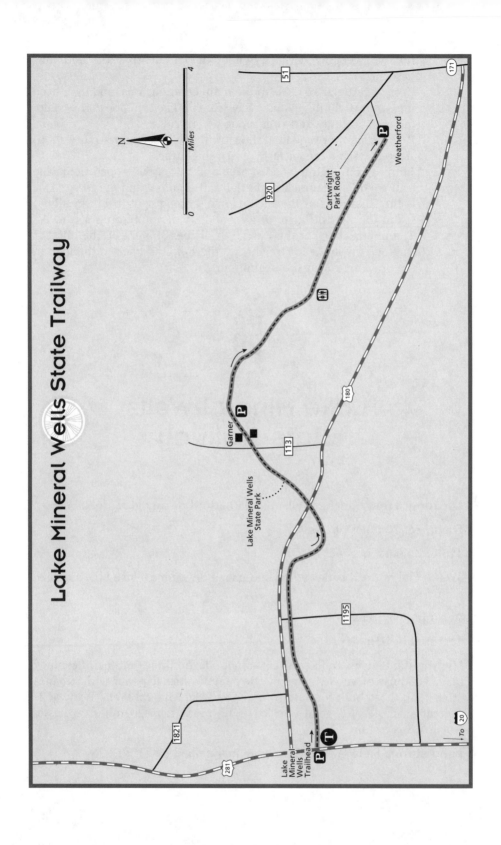

Maps: Free map available from park headquarters at Lake Mineral Wells State Park; USGS Mineral Wells West, Mineral Wells East, Garner, Weatherford North.

Access: There are four trailheads along this trailway. The Mineral Wells trailhead is on Fifth Street, just east of U.S. 281, 0.2 mile south of its intersection with U.S. 180. The Lake Mineral Wells State Park trailhead is in the state park, east about 5 miles on U.S. 180 from U.S. 281, then north on Park Road 71. In the park, proceed past the headquarters and keep to your right, following the road as it bends south then east until you reach the trailhead. There is also a trailhead in Garner, reachable off FM 113 north from U.S. 180 farther east from Lake Mineral Wells. For the Weatherford trailhead, all the way at the eastern end of the trail, take U.S. 180 to FM 51 north. Turn left at FM 920, take this to Cartwright Park Road, and head west to the parking lot. There are payboxes at every entrance to the trail—$2.00 for adults, $1.00 for kids and seniors, $4.00 for equestrians, at the time of writing.

Notes on the trail: Abandoned as uneconomical in 1992, the old Texas & Pacific line running from Weatherford to Mineral Wells sat idle for years until its grand opening in 1998 as the Lake Mineral Wells State Trailway. The path was evened out and surfaced with crushed and screened limestone, providing Texans with a quiet and beautiful avenue for exploring the land where the Comanche roamed and Charlie Goodnight ranched.

The Ride

The trailhead in Weatherford is a couple hundred feet higher up than the trailhead in Mineral Wells, but taking into consideration the wind and the slightly rolling terrain, it doesn't matter a whole lot which way you go—unless of course you're only going one-way. In that case follow the wind. I've marked the ride from Lake Mineral Wells to Weatherford.

Starting from this end, the first 5 miles run alongside a road, and then you cross U.S. 180 on a huge concrete bridge. Not the most peaceful or scenic part of the trip, but the crossings are well marked and you're separated from auto traffic. This part is also easily skipped by starting at Lake Mineral Wells State Park. At about 5.8 miles, pass the spur to Lake Mineral Wells State Park, about two-thirds of a mile away. By this time the trail has wandered away from the road and you're treated to the feel of an empty country road rolling through horse and cattle ranches along Rock Creek.

At the 8.5-mile mark the trail passes over the Dry Creek Bridge, a converted railroad bridge (you can still see the holes from the spikes). Now the trail is lined with and often sheltered by stands of oak and maple trees; you may even see the occasional roadrunner scooting along the trail. A few miles later the trail begins a slow, rolling ascent to its high point, at around 16 miles, of 1,235 feet. There's even a sign and a bench to mark the spot. From here on out, the path passes by the back reaches of some farms and plenty of flat, empty country before heading into Weatherford. A rest room, a paybox, a water fountain, and a parking lot mark the end of the trail.

While the trailway is a long one, the lack of difficulty makes it not unreasonable to do as an out-and-back. With two cars, placing one at either end, making it a one-way trip would be pretty easy as well.

Cross Timbers Trail

Location: Lake Mineral Wells State Park, Mineral Wells.

Distance: 5 miles.

Time: 30 minutes.

Tread: Mostly doubletrack.

Aerobic level: Easy.

Technical difficulty: 2.

Highlights: Multiuse, mainly equestrian trail in a very nice campground offers a good ride for beginning mountain bikers.

Land status: State Park, maintained by TPWD; fees apply.

Maps: Free map at park headquarters; USGS Mineral Wells East.

Access: From U.S. 281, take U.S. 180 east for about 5 miles. Head north on Park Road 71 to the park entrance. Inside the park, proceed past the headquarters and take your first left. Follow this road around to the Cross Timbers camping area and turn left there. The parking lot is at the very end of the road, past the loop that goes to the campsites.

Notes on the trail: It's obvious from the get-go that the primary users of the Cross Timbers Trail are of the six-legged variety—human on horseback, that is. The trail is trenched with hoofprints in many places, and if there's been any rain lately, you can bet the bike that there'll be plenty of vast, deep puddles blocking the way. But as TPWD searches for new groups of people to bring into the state parks, trails like these have been opened to bikers.

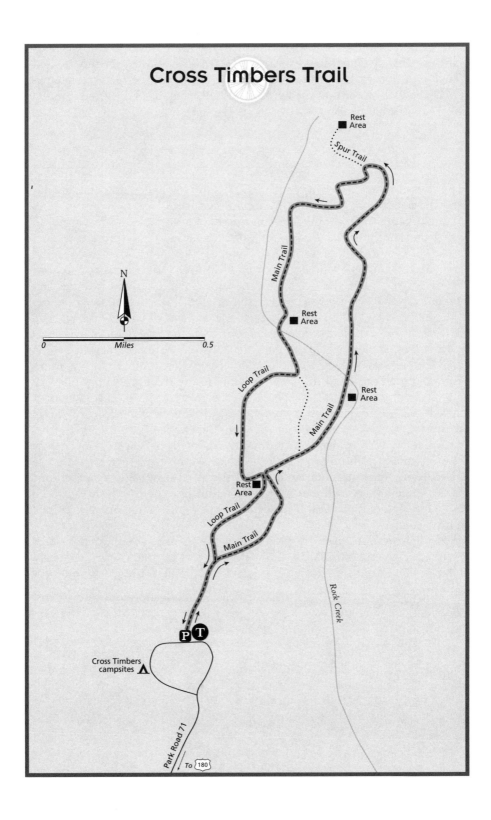

Cross Timbers Trail

N

0   Miles   0.5

Rest
Area

Spur Trail

Main Trail

Rest
Area

Loop Trail

Rest
Area

Main Trail

Rest
Area

Loop Trail

Main Trail

Rock Creek

P T

Cross Timbers
campsites

Park Road 71

To 180

The Mineral Wells area was inhabited by the Comanche until uber-rancher Charlie Goodnight ran 'em off to make room for longhorns, and ranching has been big business ever since. But it was the restorative powers of the well water that made Mineral Wells famous and turned it into a world-renowned health resort.

The Ride

The Cross Timbers is a pretty nice trail. It's not so challenging—not at all—and it's not so long, but Lake Mineral Wells State Park is a pretty, quiet chunk of land, the camping facilities are quite nice, and it's a great spot to bring the family or the newbie buddies for an easy, enjoyable ride. Just make sure you ride here during a dry spell. Unlike most other parks in the area, Lake Mineral Wells does not close its trails after a rain—and staff probably won't tell you what kind of condition this trail's in either. So when I say that this place is no fun in the mud, I speak from experience.

The trail is laid out as three loops connected sort of end to end. Signage is limited and not always very clear, but with the exception of one footpath (which *is* clearly marked), all the trails out here are open to bikers, hikers, and horses alike. I rode it counterclockwise, combining the Main Trail and the Loop Trail in one go, staying to the right at just about every intersection. I wouldn't say this is the best way to do it, but I doubt it makes much difference either way. The trail is wide almost everywhere; the terrain is easy, from flat to rolling; and traffic is pretty limited.

The Main Trail is bisected at about its midpoint by Rock Creek, with a rest area near both crossing points. There are also rest areas where the Main Trail meets the Loop Trail and at the northernmost end of the Spur Trail. There's not much elevation change out here to speak of, but there are a few gradual hills that'll make you work a little going up and *yeehaw!* a little going down.

Another thing to keep in mind is that the 22-mile Lake Mineral Wells State Trailway has a trailhead at the other end of this park. It's a nice long hike-and-bike trail that goes all the way to Weatherford (see Ride 36 for details).

38

Northshore Trail

Location: Flower Mound, on Lake Grapevine.

Distance: 15 miles out and back.

Time: 1.5 hours.

Tread: Mostly singletrack.

Aerobic level: Moderate.

Technical difficulty: 3.

Highlights: This is Dallas's most-used trail, and for good reason. A long stretch of hard-packed singletrack that winds through some gorgeous woodland, the Northshore Trail offers riding hospitable to anyone brave enough to hop in the saddle. The climbs are short, and the rough spots are not too rough.

Land status: The land is owned by the U.S. Army Corps of Engineers and maintained by the city of Flower Mound.

Maps: A decent map is available from the ACOE headquarters on FM 2499 just north of TX 121; a rough map is available on the DORBA Web site; USGS Lewisville West, Grapevine.

Access: Take I–35E north of Dallas to FM 3040. Go west 5 miles to FM 2499 and turn left. Proceed south about 1.5 miles to Long Prairie Road and turn right. The park entrance is 1 mile ahead on the right. Keep to the right on the park roads; the trailhead is all the way at the end, on the shore of Lake Grapevine.

Notes on the trail: The difficulty rating for this trail is a tough one to judge, as the Northshore Trail offers riding of many levels. Flat and twisty hardpack is perfect for beginners to get their legs and for experienced riders to test theirs, and a few of the steep drops and quick climbs should be tackled by knowledgeable hammerheads only. The trail is a pleasant and ridable one for most of the way, but there are a few spots that call for caution. The rough stuff is easily passable on foot, so don't let it discourage you from riding here. Just walk those spots until you feel comfortable enough to ride them.

Northshore Trail

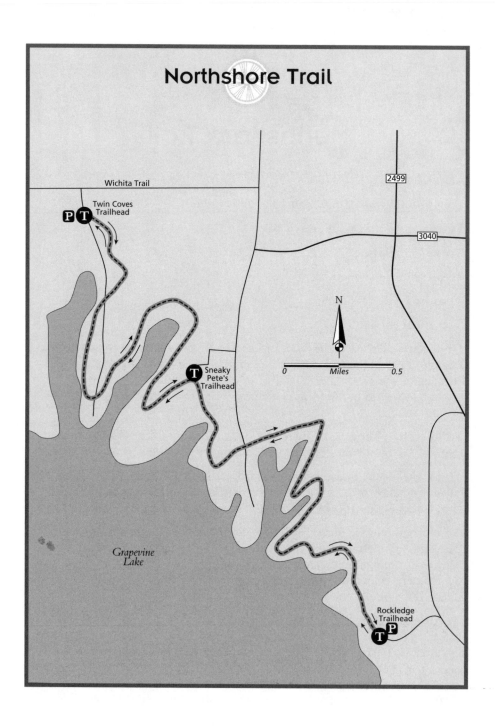

Wichita Trail

Twin Coves
Trailhead

2499

3040

N

0   Miles   0.5

Sneaky
Pete's
Trailhead

Grapevine
Lake

Rockledge
Trailhead

Keith shows us how to handle the roots and rocks at the Northshore Trail.

For the most part this trail is hard-packed singletrack that's narrow as it races through the trees and wide at hard corners and overused passing points. This trail was once used mostly by motocross riders, so much of the damage had already been done by the time mountain bikers arrived as a major use group. But bike traffic does have an impact, and it has taken its toll here. Considering that this trail sees nearly a thousand riders a week on a good week, though, it's held up remarkably well—due in no small part to the maintenance efforts of DORBA. Good job, guys. If you ride here a lot, consider joining up and helping out. Regardless, ride gently: Don't widen the trail to avoid a puddle or a rock, and stay off it altogether in bad conditions.

Most important, remember at all times that this is the most used trail in an area of very well used trails. The traffic out here on weekends is staggering: flocks of mountain bikes as well as big crowds of hikers all out for a stroll in the woods. And while you might see the foot traffic as a nuisance that slows you down or makes you stop once in a while, many hikers see a mountain biker flying blindly around a corner as a sure means of a speedy and painful death. Be nice. Advance notice is the key to avoiding collisions and nasty encounters, so call out your presence around corners and up or down hills. If you can, ride at off-times. That way you can open it up a little bit without endangering yourself or anyone else. If you can't, just take it a bit slower, yield to hikers, and be courteous. Remember: All mountain bikers are judged by the actions of every biking individual.

OK, enough of the lecture, let's get to the ride.

The Ride

You can start this ride at a few places. I parked at the Rockledge trailhead and headed west, keeping the lake to my left, and turned back at the Twin Coves trailhead. You can ride the opposite way (though apparently Twin Coves is closed during much of the winter), or you can start in the middle at Sneaky Pete's trailhead.

Setting out from Rockledge, the trail is open, flat and pretty fast, often running right along the beach and diving back into the woods. This is also the most highly trafficked portion of the trail, so watch your speed. There are a few technical challenges along here as well—quick, rooted climbs and drops that can turn nasty if you're not prepared. In a great many places, you are riding in a trench—the trail is shaped like a U, and the sides come up a good 6 inches from the lowest point. This is not some cool bobsled-style trail design; it's the result of erosion. Be careful you don't dig a pedal in here, and stay on the main trail to keep this kind of damage to a minimum.

Just past the 2.5-mile mark you'll hit a paved road. Turn left here and follow the road for 0.5 mile or so. The route is marked with paint and the reentry onto the trail is easy to spot. This is the first of many places where the trail crosses roads, some of which are still used by cars. At these points there are metal gates with openings wide enough for a person to pass through on foot but about an inch too narrow for a bike's handlebars to fit. Apparently some riders pop wheelies through the gaps, but my riding partner wisely discouraged this, pointing out that a near miss can stop your bike dead while your body continues forward to crash into the stem and handlebars. Ouch! These are tricky spots, so the best bet is to slow to a stop, wiggle your handlebars through, and then ride again. By the third or fourth gate, you'll have the hang of it and won't even have to dismount.

At about the 4.5-mile mark you'll pass the Sneaky Pete's trailhead. You'll no doubt notice that the technical spots become more challenging as you move west along the trail, and from Sneaky Pete's west to Twin Coves, the trail is at its toughest. The drops are steeper and the climbs are rockier, and while there is generally less foot traffic at this end, there is still plenty of bike traffic, so be prepared to yield on the difficult spots. There are many rock gardens and many descents that require some fancy maneuvering to stay aboard. This part of the trail is the most fun, but it's also a bit more dangerous than the rest, so be prepared—and be careful.

At about 7.5 miles you'll hit a road at the Twin Coves area on the western end of the trail. There are picnic tables here for a quick rest before you turn around and head back. The rocks, roots, and climbs that you tackled on the way out pose a whole new set of challenges on the return trip. Remember, though, that as you get farther east the traffic will increase. It's tempting to hit the final few miles at breakneck speed as the trail flattens out, but don't give in. Ride safely and courteously, and bikers will be allowed to enjoy this park for many years to come.

Knob Hill Trail

Location: Near Roanoke, west of Flower Mound.

Distance: 11 miles out and back.

Time: 1 hour.

Tread: Mostly singletrack, some doubletrack.

Aerobic level: Moderate.

Technical difficulty: 2.

Highlights: A fairly easy ride with just a few challenging spots, Knob Hill is a fun and underused trail that feels more remote than other Dallas-area rides.

Land status: The land is under control of the U.S. Army Corps of Engineers, and the trail is maintained by volunteers from DORBA.

Maps: There are no trail maps; USGS Argyle.

Access: From I–35E north of Dallas, exit Main Street (FM 1171) in Lewisville and head west. Follow this 12 miles (the road turns into Cross Timbers along the way) to U.S. 377 and turn left. The parking area for the trailhead is less than 1 mile ahead on the left, just after the first bridge. You'll head out through the brown metal gate to the right of the parking area.

Notes on the trail: Though there are a few spots within the opening mile of this trail that feel like a BMX course, it levels out and offers a nice, fast, nearly traffic-free ride through a peaceful hardwood forest and along Denton and White's Branch Creeks. Apparently there have been attempts to connect this trail to the Northshore Trail on Lake Grapevine, but those dreams are still unfulfilled at the time of writing. At the far end of the trail there's even a sign that says it *is* the Northshore Trail, but it's not.

But it *is* fun, and much of it is flat. The two or three steep spots require caution, and one of them may even call for a dismount, but for the most part the trail can be tackled by beginners with no problems. One of the best things about this trail is the relative isolation it offers. My ride here was by far the most "away from it all" I've felt on any visit to Dallas. Even on the bigger bike trails it feels like a highway or strip mall is just out of

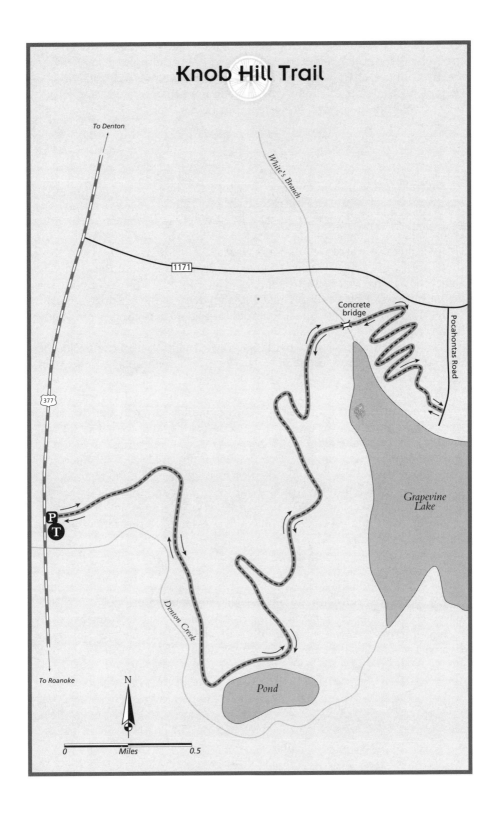

Knob Hill Trail

To Denton

White's Branch

1171

Concrete
bridge

Pocahontas Road

377

Grapevine
Lake

P
T

Denton Creek

To Roanoke

N

Pond

0   Miles   0.5

sight, but here it's quiet and unpopulated and relatively trash free. Though the lack of traffic will tempt you to take the flats at top speed, keep an eye and ear out for other bikers and for hikers. It's an out-and-back ride, so there is oncoming traffic, and when I rode here there were a couple people out walking their dogs. So go fast, but be careful.

The Ride

At the trailhead you have to carry your bike through a metal gate to get to the trail, which starts out in the open and quickly dives into an area thick with oak and cedar. The trail is very twisty and traverses a few dry creekbeds on steep lines. Be careful here. One or two of the drops are steep enough to warrant walking or at least extreme caution. The rest of them are fun and fast blasts of elevation on an otherwise flat trail. The sight lines in here are pretty good, so you shouldn't get too much surprise traffic, but be watchful just the same. An off-leash dog (which is perfectly fine with me) almost upended me on a drop in here, so I know it can happen.

You'll leave these woods on a long climb (about 30 feet) before loafing up and down a couple of small hills. The trail is well marked and there aren't too many offshoots, so finding your way is not an issue. After these hills, at about the 2.5-mile mark, the trail goes flat. And I mean flat. It winds back and forth and crosses a couple shallow ditches, but this is big ring spinning time. Work on those cornering skills, and enjoy the space.

At about the 5-mile mark you'll pass over a concrete bridge and then hit another forested section, this time very flat. In another 0.5 mile you'll come to the end of the trail and the NORTHSHORE sign. There are trails that lead out from here, but they're marked for horses and hikers only, so this is where you turn around. Take your time; enjoy the quiet and the solitude out here. And come back. This trail could use some traffic—and other area trails could use less.

Cedar Hill State Park Trail

Location: Cedar Hill State Park, near Duncanville.

Distance: 11-mile loop.

Time: 1.5 hours.

Tread: Mostly singletrack.

Aerobic level: Moderate to strenuous.

Technical difficulty: 4.

Highlights: This ride has everything. Speedy flats, climbs of all lengths and intensities, and some roller-coastery downhills that will test the limits of your tire tread are all assembled for your enjoyment at Cedar Hill State Park. There are also some great views and a large section of land being restored to its native prairie state—fantastic ride in a beautiful park just outside Dallas.

Land status: State Park.

Maps: Free park map; USGS Cedar Hill, Britton.

Access: Take I–35E south from downtown Dallas to I–20 and head west about 9 miles to FM 1382. Turn left here, at the CEDAR HILL STATE PARK sign, and follow FM 1382 about 4 miles to the park entrance on the right. Past headquarters, turn left at the stop sign (there is no sign to indicate where the bike trail begins). Follow this road awhile, past the Penn Farm, and turn left at the stop sign by the boat ramp. There's a parking area right by the trailhead at the road's end.

Notes on the trail: There may be less than 150 vertical feet separating the highest and lowest points in the park, but your legs will certainly insist that you've covered far more than that by the end of a ride here. The trail makes great use of the park's 1,400 acres, using every hill and ridge to make the ride more challenging. Kudos to DORBA and the state park staff for working together to make such a great trail. And the terrain, on the White Rock Escarpment, is absolutely beautiful. From the grassy prairies to the cedar-studded hillsides to the peaceful shores of Lake Joe Pool, Cedar Hill is an oasis in the midst of urban sprawl.

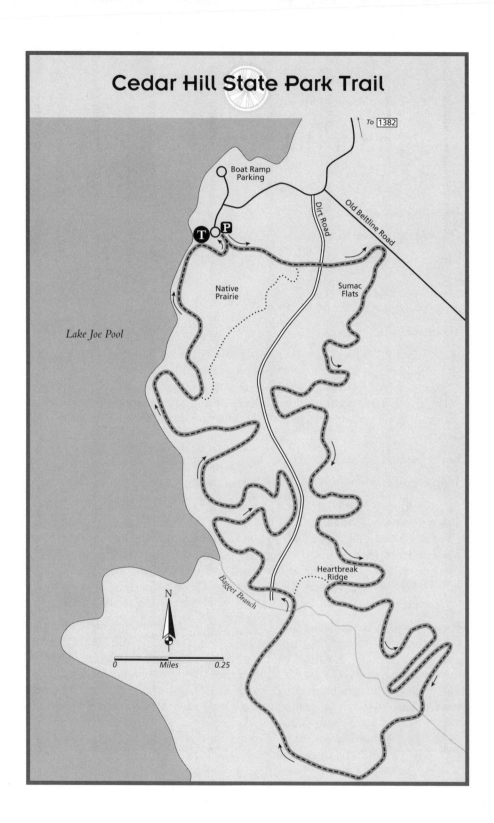

Cedar Hill State Park Trail

To 1382

Boat Ramp Parking

Dirt Road

Old Beltline Road

T P

Native Prairie

Sumac Flats

Lake Joe Pool

Bagget Branch

Heartbreak Ridge

N

0   Miles   0.25

They say the DORBA trail at Cedar Hill State Park is the best trail in this part of the state. Who am I to argue?

This trail sees plenty of traffic, but as it's a one-way loop, you can ride all day out here and only see a few other bikers. There are a few options for riders of different levels or for piecing together multiple loops. There's a 2.5-mile loop that circles the prairie area, as well as a 7.5-mile loop for intermediate riders. The trail I've marked here is the full deal, 11 miles of dynamite singletrack that'll keep a rider of *any* level happy. There are some tough spots along the expert loop, but nothing so treacherous as to scare away the midlevel rider looking for thrills and miles. The steep climbs and quick descents along the ridges before the expert turnoff are good indication of what the expert loop is like.

Abundant cedars and oaks make much of this trail nice and shady enough even for a summer ride, but long stretches are totally exposed both in the prairie and along the lakeshore. Weather is a consideration here, and, of course, if it's wet stay away. Trails used this much cannot sustain the harsh effects of yahoos who insist on riding muddy trails. In fact, the Cedar Hill State Park staff is quick to close the trails if there's been any moisture—and I mean *any* moisture. So be sure to call before taking a road trip to ride here.

The Ride

The trailhead is located at the far end of the last parking lot on the road. Head out past the sign and stay to the left at the intersections to follow the proper direction. You'll be climbing right off the bat, heading up the hill into the trees and away from the lake. Less than a mile in, you'll hit the first turnoff for the 2.5-mile loop around the native prairie. Stay left here. The short trail is not necessarily easy—there's plenty of climbing and a couple nice drops on it—but it is short.

Some long uphills take you quickly to the heights of the park, and from there you'll fall and rise and fall again in rapid succession, covering the park's elevation quickly and repeatedly. There are plenty of flat areas and smooth downhills along the way to catch your breath, so keep spinning instead of grabbing that tree at the top of the climbs. Many of the hilly sections are dug in pretty deep, forming U-shaped troughs that get you moving quickly and smoothly. Watch out, though, as the sides of these ruts can grab a pedal and send you flying. Trust me on that one.

At about the 6-mile mark there's another intersection. A right turn sends you back toward the trailhead on the intermediate loop, and a left takes you farther out on the expert loop. The expert loop is pretty tricky, with loads of steep ups and downs and more than a few ridgeline trails, but it's not a whole lot worse than what you've already ridden. Use your best judgment—then ride the whole thing! A few intense ridge traverses lead you around and over the Baggett Branch and into a long section of open prairie. There's a fast downhill here, which brings you past where the intermediate trail reconnects before sending you up another long climb.

Before too long the trail will approach the shoreline and then stay right alongside it before turning back inland for a turn around the restored prairie. This is a beautiful and exposed stretch of trail that'll have you rushing for cover or craving a dip in the lake, depending on the weather. One last bend into the woods brings you back to the original intersection, and a final left turn takes you back to the parking lot.

Cedar Brake Trail

Location: Glen Rose, southwest of Fort Worth.

Distance: 7-mile loop, with opportunity for more.

Time: 1 hour plus.

Tread: Mostly solid singletrack, with some doubletrack.

Aerobic level: Strenuous.

Technical difficulty: 4.

Highlights: These trails don't see nearly the traffic that their quality warrants, so odds are you'll have some peace and quiet for your shredding pleasure. And don't forget to check out the five or six sets of big dinosaur tracks on the edge of the riverbed.

Land status: State Park.

Maps: Free park map; USGS Hill City, Glen Rose West.

Access: From I–35W south of Fort Worth, take U.S. 67 west to Glen Rose. Turn north on FM 205 and follow it 3 miles to Park Road 59. Turn right. Past the headquarters where the road hits a T, follow the road to the right, turning right again to the parking area for the Cedar Brake Trail. The trail begins on the path to the walk-in campsites.

Notes on the trail: The trails are well marked and offer ample opportunity to change up the routes as well as plenty of gorgeous views of the landscape surrounding the Paluxy River. Watch out, though, as there are lots of unmarked trails that crisscross the main ones. If you're following the loop, just be patient and look for the markers. Familiarity is the only

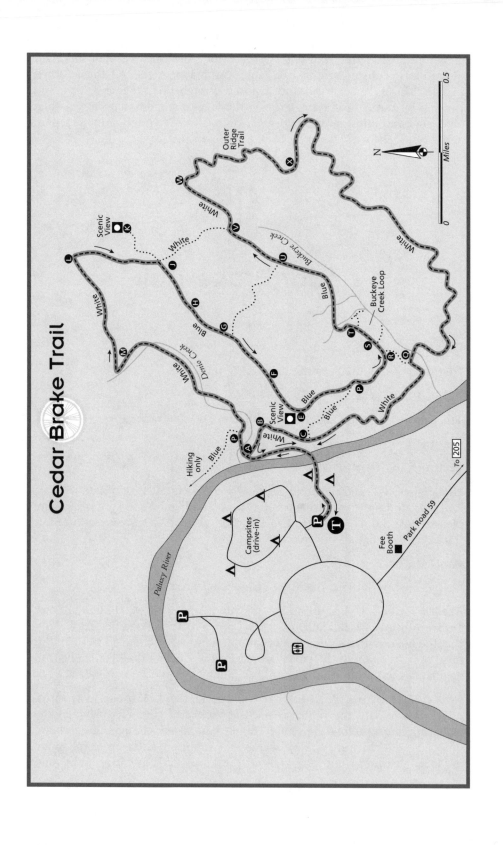

Cedar Brake Trail

Now that's what I call a shredder! His kind might be long gone from the Cedar Brake, but MTBers will be around here for a long time to come. Thank goodness that fence is between him and my bike.

way to ensure a loop free of wrong turns, so enjoy the unintentional diversions and keep on riding.

At the very beginning of the ride, you have to cross the river, stepping from rock to rock. You might get wet. The first sections of trail are especially heavy with unmarked cross-trails. Just watch for the white paint on the trees and the colored markers at the true intersections. Get the park's free map before you set out; it'll help you know what colors to look for and when.

There are some nasty drops out here, and some of them come up on you pretty suddenly. Keep your eyes ahead and your weight ready to shift back, and there'll be no worries.

The Ride

0.0 Parking area. The walk-in campsites are pretty cool. Follow the trail to the river, dismount, and hop your way across. On the other side, the trail heads up to the left, sandy and steep. Remount, and pump those legs.

0.3 Go left at the first marked intersection and right at the second, staying on the white-marked trail and heading northeast on the Denio Creek Trail. The trail crosses the creekbed several times at the beginning, and although it was dry when I rode it, there is a possibility of a wet crossing here.

1.0 Take a sharp right away from the creek, still following the white markers, and start climbing. Most of the terrain is packed tight enough to keep you moving, but some very steep sections and patches of loose rock make following a good line most beneficial.

1.3 Here's where it might start to get confusing. Keep to the right as you come up on the marker for campsite L, then head down the hill, following the trail south to the intersection with the blue trail. Some unmarked paths can lead you out and around the park's perimeter (these do reconnect, but the way is less certain and less fun). Hit the blue trail after about a quarter mile and turn right.

2.0 At the marker for campsite G, the yellow trail breaks to the left. Stay straight on the blue trail, which turns into the ridge trail and opens up on some stellar views down around campsite E.

2.5 At the marker for campsite P, the blue trail cuts back hard to the right—keep straight on the yellow trail until it connects with the next blue trail, then go left.

2.7 At campsite S, the Buckeye Creek Loop heads off to the right. This is a very scenic tour through and along the creekbed—a nice spot for a break, but not the best riding in the park. It's definitely more for hikers. Continue on the blue trail past campsite T and back up the blue trail until it runs into the white trail. This is a long winding stretch with some nice little climbs and drops, very rider-friendly for the most part.

3.3 The blue trail ends at a T with the white trail. Turn right, climbing out to the marker for campsite W, where you'll connect with the Outer Ridge Trail.

3.6 This is one of the fastest, most fun sections out here—a high-speed, momentum-driven stretch that skirts the outer edge of the park, leading you back down toward the Paluxy River.

4.0 Continue past campsite X, flying around the bermed curves and over the bumps, climbing and descending through the thick cedars until you cross Buckeye Creek at about 5.2 miles and then reach the intersection at campsite Q.

5.3 Turn left at campsite Q and follow the River Trail northwest. Lots of unmarked trails lead off on both sides down here, but stick to the main trail, which leads to campsite C and another scenic overlook.

6.1 Stay on the white trail as you pass campsite C, another quarter of a mile until you reach campsite A, which is the intersection you hit at the very beginning. To get back across the river, turn left, or take a right to reconnect with the Denio Creek Trail to have another go at the course.

6.5 Campsite A, turn left and follow the trail back down to the river. You've been here before. Cross the river, climb up the other bank toward the walk-in campsites, and you're on your way back to the parking lot. Either way around the campsite path will lead you to the lot.

Cleburne State Park Trail

Location: 10 miles southwest of Cleburne.

Distance: 7-mile loop.

Time: 1 hour.

Tread: Mostly hard-packed singletrack, with a couple miles' worth of doubletrack.

Aerobic level: Moderate.

Technical difficulty: 3.

Highlights: The beginning section of this ride offers some fun technical challenges, and there are plenty of scenic views of Cedar Lake when the bike trail hooks up with the nature trail.

Land status: State Park.

Maps: Free park map; USGS Cleburne West.

Access: From I–35W south of Fort Worth, take U.S. 67 west past Cleburne to Park Road 21. Turn left and follow the road 6 miles to park headquarters. From there, proceed past the baseball fields on your right just a few yards to the first rest rooms on your left. Park here; the trailhead is a few more yards up the road on the left.

Notes on the trail: When I visited Cleburne State Park, the bike trails were in, shall we say, a state of flux. The outer loop had taken shape nicely, but the rest seemed to be suffering from "too many cooks spoiling the soup" syndrome, as the open space between either end of the main loop was laced with homemade shortcuts and crisscrosses. I soon found that these unmarked fledgeling trails led only to one another, providing some fun little hills and turns but seemingly doing more harm than good. So I stuck to the perimeter loop, and until the interior maze is marked (and approved, of course), you might want to do the same.

This loop is definitely a mixed bag. At the outset there are some beautifully twisted stretches of hard-packed singletrack snaking through dense tree cover and clearing some fairly steep drops and climbs. And though the return portion of the loop was somewhat boring, mostly following the fenceline up and down a series of hills and washes, it will keep your climbing legs warm.

Cleburne State Park Trail

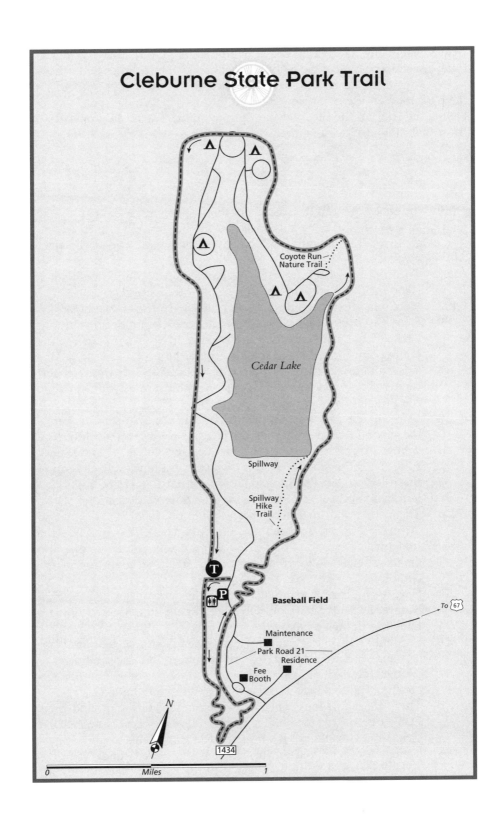

Coyote Run Nature Trail

Cedar Lake

Spillway

Spillway Hike Trail

T

P

Baseball Field

To 67

Maintenance

Park Road 21
Residence

Fee
Booth

N

1434

0   Miles   1

Near the spillway, at about Mile 2, the trail is tough to follow—the logical thing seems to be to take the spillway trail across the width of Cedar Lake to the west. *Don't do it.* This cuts the ride in half and dumps you out on the park road on the other side. Keep to the right before the spillway, following the trail up the bluff on the right to connect with the upper trail. After that, it's fairly well marked.

The Ride

0.0   Trailhead, just up the road from the rest rooms on the left, by the TEXAS LIME QUARRY sign. Once you hit the fenceline, turn left on the trail. The downhill will have you moving at a good clip right away.

0.5   The trail dips back into the woods, leading up and down some steep inclines and over the first small wooden bridge.

0.7   Here's the first steep drop—watch the sharp left at the bottom.

0.9   Here's an even steeper drop. Approach with caution, get your butt back off the seat, and dive in. Then keep your eyes out for the white paint on rocks and trees marking the route.

1.4   The trail crosses the park road here, about 30 yards from the rest rooms where you parked. The next section throws you through a fun bunch of whoop-de-dos.

2.0   Crossing another wooden bridge and the creek beyond it, here's the place to keep your eyes out for the route up the bluff. The spillway offers a nice view of the lake, but you'll get better ones from the other side. Work your way up to the right to the top of the ridge, where you'll connect with a hard, gravelly trail. Turn left; head northward and look for the white paint marks.

2.6   The path leads up a long, steep limestone shelf to a sign that directs you to the Lookout and the Lake Loop. This is where the trail turns from tight and winding to a long series of ups and downs. Some of the drops are pretty steep; so are some of the climbs.

2.9   Here the Lake Loop breaks off to the left to the Coyote Run Nature Trail. It's loose, jumbly rock for a while, up and down a bunch of drainages along the fenceline.

3.7   Suddenly the trail is beautiful again—shady stretches of hard singletrack winding downhill toward the water and across a bridge to another intersection. Going straight here will take you to the Coyote Run Trailhead; stay to the right to continue the loop.

4.2   There's a whole mess of faucets sticking out of the ground here. Don't fill your water bottles, though. I don't know why, but the signs say NO DRINKING; it's best to heed this advice.

4.6   There's a picnic area on the left and the park boundary on the right. Soon the trail dumps you onto the road—at least it did last time I was out here. If it still does, cross the cul-de-sac and get back on the trail, heading straight up a rocky wash. Then you'll head back down, then up, then down, then up, over and over.

5.6 Yes, you're still going up and down, following the contour, tackling some tough climbs, and *yeehawing* your way down some fast descents. Keep it up.

6.5 At long last, you depart the trail on the park's boundary, heading to the left on some nice singletrack.

7.0 There's a T in the trail and the big sign that says TEXAS LIME QUARRY. Go left to return to the parking area, or keep straight to clock another lap.

Southeast Texas

If there's one part of this state where the riding is affected by weather more than any other, this is it. There are plenty of rides to do in the Houston area and beyond, down to the Gulf Coast and up to the more eastern regions—but not if it's been raining. *Any* ride here is pretty much unridable if there's been any moisture in the air. So be aware of trail conditions. The trails here see tons of use, and a passel of bikers would be very upset if their trails were trashed by impolite interlopers.

The centerpiece of riding here is in the middle of Houston: the trails at Memorial Park. Called the Ho Chi Minh Trail by many, this mazelike web of singletrack covers a relatively small area where Interstates 610 and 10 meet. The riding is fast and fun, and there's a surprising amount of ground to cover. Some of the trails here have been closed in recent years, which is a serious blow to area mountain bikers, so watch for and obey trail-closure signs. Outlaw riding will only hurt the chances of getting these areas reopened. Close to town, the trail at Jack Brooks Park is a fantastic though short piece of speedy singletrack, inviting riders to fly through lap after lap at time-trial pace.

The Somerville Trailway and Brazos Bend State Park are entirely different trailwise. Somerville, farther north, is flat as flat can be, winding its way between two different ends of the same state park in what is practically a road ride. Hard dirt (with some sandy sections) and long, long lines will have your legs spinning endlessly. This one is great for training—or learning—on. At Brazos Bend, just watch out for the gators. Seriously. They're as plentiful here as mosquitoes are at every other ride in the area. In other words, they're everywhere. Be careful—of the gators *and* the skeeters.

Somerville Trailway

Location: Lake Somerville State Park, from Somerville to Ledbetter.

Distance: 27 miles round-trip.

Time: 2.5 hours.

Tread: Mostly doubletrack, with some singletrack and some wide gravel path.

Aerobic level: Moderate.

Technical difficulty: 1.

Highlights: A long, easy ride through flat and piney East Texas woodlands, the Somerville Trailway connects the Birch Creek and the Nails Creek units of Lake Somerville State Park. This is a good beginner's trail, as it offers a place to put in some long miles without any serious technical challenges.

Land status: State Park and trailway, maintained by TPWD.

Maps: Free map at park headquarters; USGS Dime Box, Flag Pond, Somerville.

Access: To reach the Birch Creek Unit from Somerville, take TX 36 north for about 4 miles to Lyons. Then take TX 60 west for 8 miles to Park Road 57. Turn here and go 4 miles to the park entrance. Head right after headquarters; go all the way to the road's end and park in the circle right at the trailhead. I suggest starting at the Birch Creek end, because the last couple miles before reaching the Nails Creek access is sandy and powdery and not fun to ride in. So unless you want to go into the park at Nails Creek, you could turn around here and head back without missing too much. To begin at Nails Creek, take U.S. 290 east from Giddings to FM 180. The park is on FM 180, 15 miles northeast of U.S. 290.

Notes on the trail: The beauty of this trail is something like the beauty of the midwestern prairie—it's there, but you gotta let yourself appreciate it. Ultraflat, grassy, and stretching out as far as you can see, the open distance makes for windy days and gigantic skies. Don't be misled, though: The length of the trail and the fact that there's not much opportunity to coast make this ride deceivingly tough. You will get a workout. Bring some

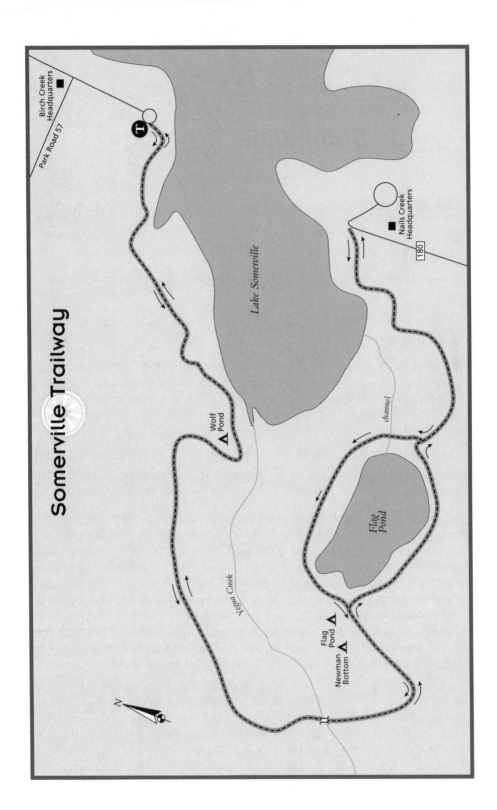

Somerville Trailway

Birch Creek Headquarters
Park Road 57

Nails Creek Headquarters
180

Lake Somerville

Wolf Pond

channel

Flag Pond

Yegua Creek

Flag Pond
Newman Bottom

N

This bridge just might be the biggest climb on the Somerville Trailway.

food, and make sure you have enough water. Water is available in the parks at both ends of the trail, but only at the ends, and it's a long way in between.

The Ride

0.0 Birch Creek trailhead.

0.7 Lake Somerville comes into view as the trail bends to the right to skirt the shore.

2.2 A small pavilion at the lake's edge is a nice spot for a break, if you are so inclined. If not, stay in that big ring and keep grinding out the miles. There's a long way to go. Some small trails cross the main trailway, and if you're not going all the way to the end and back, consider exploring these options.

3.6 Pass a couple of benches and, shortly thereafter, the Wolf Pond camp area. There's an outhouse and an arrangement of logs to sit on, and that's about it. When I was here, this was the last place I saw another living soul until I reached the other end of the trail. From here, it's flat, flat, flat.

6.8 After some time spinning in the flats, the trail dips into some trees near a dried-out pond and soon comes up on a bridge over Yegua Creek. After that there's another bridge, a small concrete one over a tiny tributary, followed by a short rocky climb.

7.7 Passing the Newman Bottom camping area, come to Flag Pond. Trails go around the pond on either side, so take one on the way out and the other on the way back. There are rest rooms near the trail junctions on either side of the pond, as well as pavilions and camping areas.

9.0 The trail around Flag Pond was pretty torn up with hoofprints when I rode here, so expect rough riding if it's dry—and much mud if it's wet. (If it's wet, find something else to do. This would not be fun in the mud.)

9.4 Suddenly the trail plunges into some gorgeous piney woods. The ground is soft and covered with needles, sandy and rocky. Keep those pedals moving!

10.5 A nice downhill throws you into some long, smooth, winding doubletrack—a perfect opportunity to open things up with an all-out sprint. That's the most fun you'll have all day.

11.0 There's a bridge right before this mile marker, and then the trail turns to powder. Sand, and lots of it, stands between you and the trailhead at the other end. Continue on if you must, but you'd be better off turning around here and skipping the 2.3 miles of this nonsense. There is some singletrack at the other end, hidden off to the side in the trees, but it only goes out away from the main trail and back just past where it left. It doesn't spare you any of the sand.

13.3 Nails Creek Unit, the end. Now, turn around and head back.

16.7 Here's the Flag Pond split. The hiking loops are nice diversions—but if it's easy, continued riding you want, stick to the bike path.

20.4 Back again at the Yegua Creek bridge.

23.5 Wolf Pond camping area—almost back!

26.1 The lake appears again to your right.

27.1 Back at the trailhead.

Memorial Park

Location: Houston.

Distance: 6-mile loop.

Time: 1 hour.

Tread: Mostly singletrack.

Aerobic level: Moderate.

Technical difficulty: 3.

Highlights: Smack-dab in the middle of the third biggest city in the nation is this beautiful park full of really fun singletrack. A jogging path and soccer and baseball fields make this park a prime athlete's destination, but the bike trails are the main attraction here. Tight, zigzagging, tree-shaded singletrack that winds around on itself for miles means hours of fun just out of sight of the skyline.

Land status: City Park.

Maps: USGS Houston Heights.

Access: From north of Houston, take Loop 610 west to the Woodway/ Memorial exit and head east. Turn right at Picnic Lane, just after the railroad overpass. Park in the lots near the baseball fields or wherever it is legal and you can find space.

Notes on the trail: Do *not* ride this trail if it's wet. You will wreck it— and it will wreck you. This trail has been dubbed the Ho Chi Minh Trail, and old Uncle Ho would have felt right at home in the junglelike environs of this lush urban park.

If it's dry, get set to have yourself a blast. Though I've listed this as a 6-mile loop, there are more than 6 miles of trail out here, and it's not much of a loop. I've always thought that the best way to ride this place is to follow someone who knows it well. In lieu of that, I think the best thing would be to try your hardest to get lost. You won't be able to, as the park is bordered by major roads or a waterway all around, but you'll avoid repeating trail sections and will more likely explore the entire park.

The trails themselves are mostly singletrack, though they're getting wider all the time with use. Hard-packed dirt in an endless series of

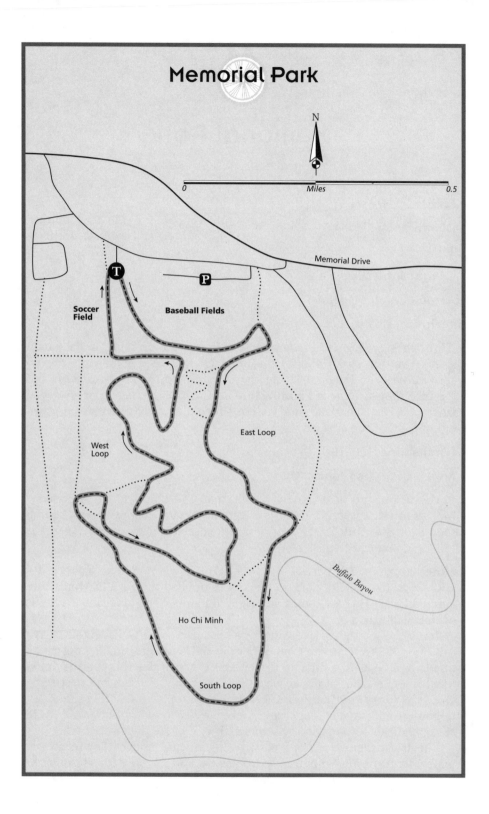

whoop-de-dos and short, steep climbs and drops are the orders of the day here, and an assortment of rocks and roots that get bigger with the years offer some technical challenges that could unseat you if you're not careful.

As you'd expect from a park like this in a city this size, the traffic out here is heavier than I've seen on any other bike trail. Be careful and watch for oncoming traffic, or you could end up in a world of hurt, and so could someone else.

The Ride

The Ho Chi Minh Trail occupies the southwest corner of the park, butting up against Buffalo Bayou along the south border, and extends north to encompass in a large loop a series of smaller singletrack loops that are not all so well marked. The trails are color-coded—red, yellow, green and blue in descending order of difficulty, I think—but it's likely you'll still have a little trouble finding your way around at first.

There are many more trails here, but last I checked the Cambodia Trail and the Laos Trail were closed to bikes due to erosion. If there are signs marking trails closed, obey them. There are tons of cyclists in Houston who cannot afford to lose access to Memorial Park. So don't blow it for them.

Enter the Ho Chi Minh Trail off Memorial Drive near the soccer fields and head south to a series of singletrack loops. No doubt you'll find that you're riding in circles, but you will recognize intersections and remember which bits lead off in which direction, and that's the first step in learning your way around. Beyond this multitude of loops, the main trail takes a big, wide turn against the shore of Buffalo Bayou on the park's south border, and there are some pretty tricky spots down here. Drops are surprisingly steep, and the climbs are fairly tough for an area with practically no elevation gain whatsoever.

When you're done and you find yourself back at the beginning, do it all over again. Odds are there are some trails out there you missed the first time around.

Brazos Bend State Park

Location: Near Richmond, one hour south of Houston.

Distance: 8-mile loop.

Time: 45 minutes.

Tread: Wide gravel path, some road, little singletrack.

Aerobic level: Easy.

Technical difficulty: 1.

Highlights: A good trip for the whole family, with practically no elevation change and all smooth surfaces. Gator sightings are likely here as well, so if you do bring the kids, keep an eye on them.

Land status: State Park.

Maps: Free park map; USGS Smithers Lake, Thompsons, Damon, and Otey.

Access: From Houston, take U.S. 59 south to Richmond, and then head south on FM 762. Take this 20 miles to the park road. Past headquarters, park in the first parking area you see on your left. The trail begins to the right of the rest rooms, across a small wooden bridge.

Notes on the trail: Two words: pan cake. This trail is so flat it could have given Columbus pause. But that doesn't mean that a spin around the lakes at Brazos Bend State Park doesn't offer its own rewards. For the most part the trail is a wide, level gravel path that runs along elevated embankments next to the lakes and sloughs that make up the park's interior. The easy terrain and the gorgeous scenery—green swampy meadows and trees filled with Spanish moss—make this the perfect family ride. The trail is a connected series of loops, so you can ride as short or as long as you want.

The main path that I outline here wanders around 40 Acre, Elm, and Hale Lakes—all of which are prime spots for alligator sightings. Of course, be careful. The beasts seem peaceful enough, but there is little besides a bit of bank separating you from them at most points on this trail. Watch the kids and, like the signs in the park say, DON'T HARASS THE ALLIGATORS.

There are more trails, too, that go beyond Hale Lake and down to the Brazos River. Be courteous to hikers, as they're definitely the prime users of these trails.

Brazos Bend State Park

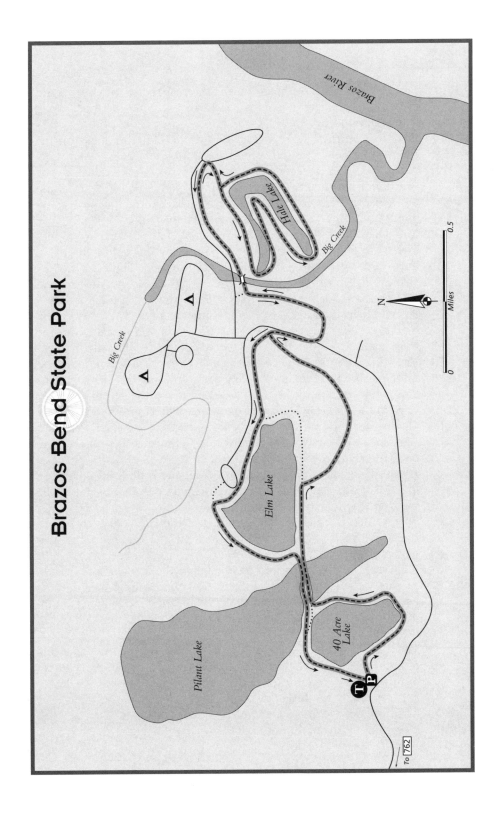

The Ride

0.0 From the parking lot, head toward the rest rooms and veer right, crossing a wooden bridge and following a wide dirt path away from the building.

0.3 First fork; turn right to follow this route. Skirt the lakes on the right on the way out and come back on the left side.

1.0 An observation tower offers a good view of 40 Acre Lake on the southwest and Pilant Lake to the north and east. Birds are abundant in this park, and this tower affords one of the best views you'll find. Turn right, cutting across Pilant Lake.

1.6 Elm Lake Trail. Turn right again, keeping the lake to your left. There are plenty of great fishing spots along this side of the lake.

2.5 Turn right when the trail comes up to the road. There's a narrow strip of dirt to ride on just to the side of the road, or you can just ride on the road. When the road splits in about 0.5 mile, follow it left and then right again at the next intersection. You'll see Creekfield Lake to your right, and just after that you can pick up the trail again. The singletrack here is winding and pleasant.

3.5 The trail meets the road again at Big Creek, and there is a footbridge as well as the auto bridge. After crossing the bridge, take a hard right back onto the trail and head toward Hale Lake.

3.8 The trail splits; stay right and circle the lake counterclockwise.

4.0 On the left, a spur trail leads to Hale Lake Lookout Point for another excellent view of the swampy environs. It's an out-and-back trail with a little loop at the end.

4.6 A trail heads off to the right, away from the Hale Lake Loop. Follow this if you want the extra miles of trail on the other side of the road, or stay left to return to the main loop.

5.0 Back at the junction at the beginning of the Hale Lake loop. Turn right and head back to the Big Creek Bridge for the return trip home.

5.3 Big Creek Bridge, cross and head back to the left along the road.

5.8 At the second paved road intersection the parking area for the park's observatory is around the bend on the road heading south. A visit here and to the Challenger Learning Center are well worth the delay.

6.3 The trail forks; staying to the right takes you around the north side of Elm Lake. This is a well-used stretch of trail so, like everywhere in this park, watch out for and yield the right of way to pedestrians, especially the little ones.

7.0 Trail junction; turn right and cross Pilant Lake.

7.6 Observation tower, 40 Acre Lake, turn right again.

8.1 Back at the parking lot.

Southeast Texas Honorable Mention

(H) Jack Brooks Park

Location: Hitchcock, between Houston and Galveston.

Distance: 5 miles.

Time: 30 minutes.

Tread: Mostly singletrack, connected by doubletrack.

Aerobic level: Moderate.

Technical difficulty: 2.

Highlights: A short track with no major climbs, this tight and twisty trail can be an easy lope in the woods or a high-speed test of skill, depending on what you're up for when you visit.

Land status: Owned by the Galveston County Beach Park Board.

Maps: Maps are tough (or impossible) to come by, but not really necessary; USGS Hitchcock.

Access: Take I-45 south from Houston to FM 2004 (exit 15). Turn right and head south on FM 2004 for 3 miles, passing the Gulf Greyhound Park, to the entrance of Jack Brooks Park. Park by the Veteran's Memorial Pavilion; the trailhead is clearly marked.

Notes on the trail: If there's even the most remote possibility that someone has spit on this trail in the last couple days, *do not ride here.* My first attempt was a day after a rain, and it was cut short—very short. The mud gets thick and inescapable, and that's nothing a responsible individual should be attempting. But when it's dry, it's a blast. A nice canopy of trees covers most of the trail, but some of it is exposed—and all of it is home to swarms of mosquitoes and some gigantic, bright blue spiders that seem to prefer building their webs across the trail, about head-high.

The ride: Past the trailhead sign, stick to the right-hand trail, the one that looks more rutted (the one on the left is the nature trail). The path leads out and into the trees, where you'll take a hard right turn into the heavier woods. Right off the bat you'll be throwing yourself up and over some quick, rooted bumps and short, steep mounds. Occasional spray-painted arrows or little wooden bike signs do a fair job of keeping you on the right track—but even if you get off the trail, there's not much room to get lost, so don't worry. Abundant cross-trails make the route a bit confusing, but the trail's so short you'll have plenty of time to figure it out.

The trail keeps on like this for the next 4 miles or so, jumping between quick sets of small hills and tight-cornered flat singletrack, forming a loop of sorts between the water barrier of the Highland Bayou and the park roads. The whole park sits at about 15 feet above sea level, so no climb will last more than a few seconds. You'll end up right back where you started—and it's almost sure you'll want to hop right back on for another lap.

East Texas

There's something sublime about a trail covered with a blanket of pine needles. Out here in East Texas, that's exactly what you'll find. The long swath of piney woods that separates the rest of the state from Louisiana and Arkansas is in many ways a biker's paradise. It may seem that it's all flat out here, but it's not. Abundant creeks and hills lie concealed behind the walls of tall pine trees, and in many areas these features are home to miles and miles of singletrack.

Without a doubt, the foremost ride in the area is at Tyler State Park. This trail, a simple and efficient design of interconnected loops, is both easy to navigate and tough to conquer. There are climbs that are surprisingly steep—one even has a long set of switchbacks that would almost make you think you were way out west—and descents that last far more than the ten seconds that you're probably used to. The sheltered, shady singletrack here challenges your technical abilities as well as your legs and lungs and provides enough trail to keep you happy for as many long-weekend visits as you can manage.

Just a bit farther east, the trails at Martin Creek Lake State Park are similar, though flatter. They offer the same terrain without the big hills, perfect for beginners and experts alike. The trails at Huntsville State Park and in the Sam Houston National Forest offer rolling hills, plenty of shade, and that wonderful bed of pine needles underwheel.

Farther toward the central region, Lake Bryan Park has a pair of loops that offer race course–style riding of varying levels. This is a great ride and one of the few serving the Texas A&M population in nearby College Station. At the other extreme, just across the border in Louisiana, Lincoln Parish Park is home to a world-class mountain bike trail—literally. The Texas Cup has its final race of the season here, which is why I've included it in this book. It's a fantastic, amazing trail that attracts the nation's best riders because it has everything you could ask for.

Though it's hot and incredibly humid out here in the warmer months, the ubiquitous pine canopy and the proximity of each of these trails to bodies of water where you can swim away the sweat make these rides more hospitable than many others in the summertime. Take a deep breath, enjoy the sharp, clean scent—and ride.

Tyler State Park

Location: Tyler.

Distance: 11-mile loop.

Time: 2 hours.

Tread: Singletrack.

Aerobic level: Moderate to strenuous.

Technical difficulty: 4.

Highlights: Climbing? In East Texas? That's right, folks, Tyler State Park has hills you'd never expect to find in this part of the state, and the fantastic trails that traverse them are among the finest miles of singletrack in Texas. It isn't easy out there, but it sure is fun.

Land status: State Park.

Maps: Free map at park headquarters; USGS Tyler North.

Access: From I–20 north of Tyler, take FM 14 north for 2 miles to the park entrance. Past headquarters, follow the split in the park road to the left and continue around to the Black Jack group camping area. The trail heads out from here.

Notes on the trail: Climbs that start fires in your legs, descents that get the tears streaming from your eyes, perfectly engineered switchbacks, and a logical routing and sign system—aside from a free keg of cold Shiner at trail's end, Tyler State Park has just about everything a Texas mountain biker could want. Plan to spend more than just a day, because once around won't be enough.

I lucked out when I rode here, as I managed to tag along with a trio of locals who were helpful, informative, and good riders all. So, to Ronnie and friends, I thank you. But if you're going it alone, or with other first-timers, fear not. The trails are marked as well as you could hope for. A series of connected loops is marked A through D, and if you simply turn left at all the junctions on the way out and on the way back, you cover all but the short connector trails and end up right where you started. Also, at any point where the loops meet on the way out, a simple right turn will get you headed back to the beginning—or the end, whichever you prefer.

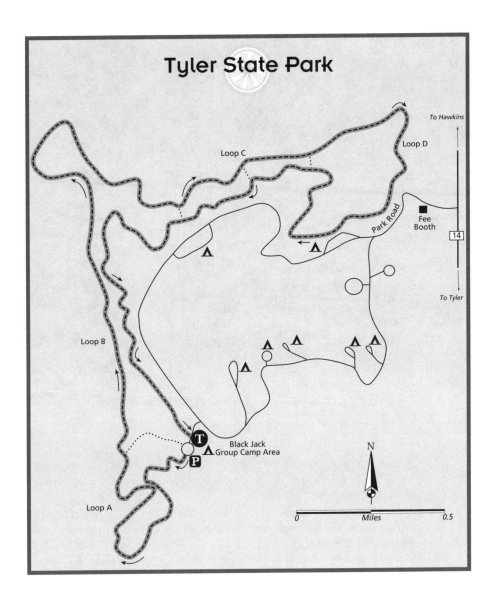

Tyler State Park

To Hawkins

Loop D

Loop C

Park Road

Fee
Booth

14

To Tyler

Loop B

Loop A

Black Jack
Group Camp Area

N

0   Miles   0.5

A bailout due to exhaustion or waning daylight is as easy as that. So, no worries.

The Ride

0.0   Right off the blocks, you're moving pretty quick—zooming out of the parking lot down a hill to start off Loop A. This is marked as a beginner's loop, and it is a pretty mild indication of what's to come.

Tyler State Park is one of the best trails in the state.

1.1   A nice, steep drop and then a quick climb back up get the blood pumping here. This leads to a longer climb before the trail planes out for some tight cornering.

2.5   A long downhill leads to another long climb. This pattern will repeat itself throughout your time here, so get into a rhythm and conserve your energy.

3.3   My last time here, this part of the trail, near the junction of Loops A and B, was pretty torn up by tractors, with big ruts and tire grooves crossing numerous times. We trudged through it, past the construction fence and up a long climb. All that should be done by the time you read this, though. Anyway, it only lasts for a quarter mile or so.

4.1   A dirt road crossing here, according to my guides, leads back to the pavilion, where you can get a burger. We didn't attempt it this day.

4.6   At the junction of Loops B and C, turn left onto C. (Or use this as a shortcut to follow the trail right down the inside half of Loop B and back to the beginning.)

4.8 This set of switchbacks is sweet. Steep corners and solid lines make for strong climbing up the sharp incline of this hill.

5.3 The downhill that follows those switchbacks brings you to the junction of Loop D, where you'll take another left. This loop is marked on the bike map as the ADVANCED LOOP. While it does perhaps have a few precipitous drops and some grueling uphills, it's really no more severe than the rest of the trails out here.

6.6 Following a number of long trips up and down a bluff on the far east end of the trail brings you around the bend and onto the journey homeward.

7.0 The marked trail skirts a really steep drop here, which the leader of our little group chose to take. It took me until my second visit to brave that sucker.

8.3 Crest of the third long climb in a row, this one higher than the others.

8.7 Junction of the inside of Loop B, followed closely by a sign indicating that you are indeed on the way back to the Black Jack parking lot. If only the way were this clear on every trail.

9.4 Hit a physical low point of the park here in a dry gully.

9.8 Steep climb!

10.2 The Loop B singletrack on the way back in is a fantastic way to end this ride. Sweeping corners and fast descents and climbs keep your momentum up and your legs moving.

10.8 Back at the Black Jack parking lot.

Martin Creek Lake State Park

Location: Tatum.

Distance: 7.5-mile loop.

Time: 1 hour.

Tread: Mostly singletrack, some doubletrack.

Aerobic level: Easy to Moderate.

Technical difficulty: 2.

Highlights: A particularly fast and curvy stretch of singletrack, the trail at Martin Creek Lake State Park is a blast for riders of any level. It's relatively flat and mostly tree covered, with ample access to the lake, so summertime rides are a definite possibility—although the hardwoods show some brilliant colors in the cooler fall months.

Land status: State Park.

Maps: Free map at park headquarters; USGS Tatum.

Access: From Tyler, take TX 64 east to Henderson. In Henderson, turn north on TX 43 toward Tatum. After 15 miles, turn right on County Road 2183—watch for the sign. The park will be on your right. Enter and proceed past the rest rooms and around the bend to the Broken Bowl camping area. Turn in to the left, and park in the area near the rest rooms. The trail begins just across the street from the rest rooms and is described here as starting with a right turn at the split and following the trail counterclockwise.

Notes on the trail: A root-laced piney woods ride that dips incessantly into creekbeds and winds around and over Old Henderson Road, this trail offers an introductory version of the best riding East Texas has to offer. It's well marked with blazes, white paint, and signs, and it's as easy to cut short as it is to churn out multiple laps.

It had rained recently when I rode these trails, so the ground was a bit sticky. It drains fairly well, though, so a little wet wouldn't make it unridable—although it would be a different story if the creek is full to running. Call and check trail conditions if it has been raining.

The trails here are only recently open to mountain bikes, so, as with any multiuse trail system, it's imperative that we be polite ambassadors of our

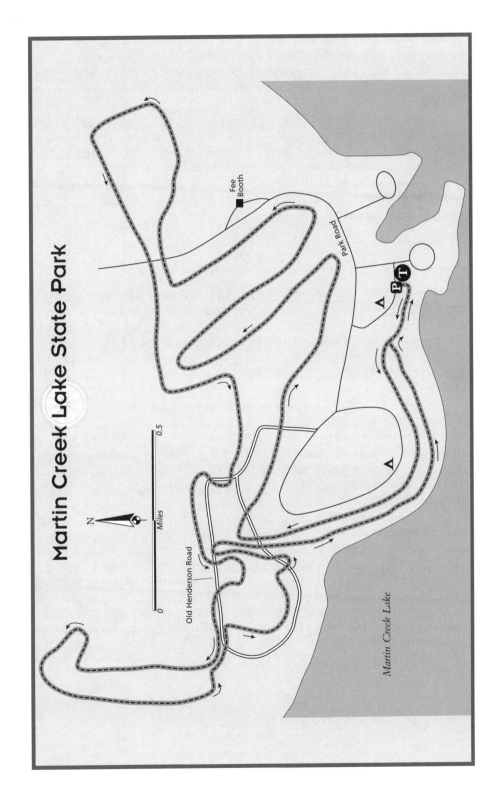

Martin Creek Lake State Park

N

Old Henderson Road

0   Miles   0.5

Fee Booth

Park Road

P T

Martin Creek Lake

sport. Ridable land is limited enough as it is in Texas, and we don't want to lose rights to places like this. Yield the trail, watch your speed, and be nice. All the folks I came across out here were sweet as punch, and it'd be a good thing for bikers to *keep* relations with runners, hikers, and walkers friendly.

Martin Creek Lake State Park is a very nice smaller counterpart to big brother Tyler State Park, which is a little under an hour to the west. The 5,000-acre lake was built to provide cooling for the lignite-fired power plant just across the water from the park, which is what creates that low "traffic hum" you'll hear all day. Regardless, this is a pretty nice place to spend a weekend—and a great place to combine with Tyler for a long weekend of camping and riding.

The Ride

From the parking area by the Broken Bowl rest rooms, take the trail out to the split and head to the right. You'll coast along some smooth trail sandwiched between the row of campsites and the lake for a while before turning away from the water and bending back around the campsites on the other side of the circle, crossing the dirt Old Henderson Road a few times along the way. This is all tight, relatively easy singletrack that dives back and forth along a couple creekbeds.

Just short of 3 miles in, you'll cross the paved park road, heading east, to do a 1-mile trail addition that's not on the free park map. There are a couple pretty hairy drops over here, short and steep, the first with a sharp turn right at the bottom. The trail is marked in one direction and is easy to follow. When you come back to the paved road, a quick left and an equally quick turnoff to the right get you back across the road to the main trail.

The western end of the park has two additional loop trails that extend beyond the bounds of Old Henderson Road (which is the path marked for hiking only). These are both ridable—some open grassy meadow and some dirt singletrack, all of it good for adding on miles. The leaves can make a pretty thick ground cover in the fall months, so watch for trail markers or you may get a bit off course. Many creek crossings and a few wooden bridges later you'll find yourself flying back along the trail between the campsites and the lake, this time with the lake to your right, at which time you can head back to the car or avoid the turnoff and do the whole thing again.

48

Lake Bryan Park

Location: Bryan.

Distance: 17 miles (8-mile loop and 9-mile loop).

Time: 2.5 hours (1 hour and 1.5 hours).

Tread: Mostly singletrack, a little doubletrack.

Aerobic level: Moderate.

Technical difficulty: 2 and 3.

Highlights: Both loops offer many miles of singletrack that wind around opposite sides of Lake Bryan. The loop that begins on the left side of the entry road (on the way into the park) is a bit easier than the newer loop that takes off from the right side, but both are fair game for riders of all levels. We can thank the Brazos Valley Mountain Bike Association for putting these trails together.

Land status: Run by the Bryan Parks and Recreation Department.

Maps: A map is available on the BVMBA Web site at bvmba.txcyber.com; USGS Bryan West.

Access: From Bryan/College Station, take FM 2818 north, past Highway 21, to Sandy Point Road. Turn left and go 3.3 miles to the park entrance on the right. The trailheads are on either side of the park road just before the entry station.

Notes on the trail: The West Loop is a little easier, a little shorter, and a little less fun than the newer East Loop, but both trails are exactly what any Saturday-ride-loving mountain biker wants: miles and miles of glorious singletrack. That's the feeling when you ride Lake Bryan Park—like there's nothing more important than a narrow dirt path, and there's plenty of it out here.

There's plenty of room to park by the boat dock, which is to your left as you enter the park; there are also campsites on the lake if you want to make an overnighter of it. When I rode here, it cost $5.00 to ride and $10.00 to camp. Traffic through the park can be pretty heavy, and people come and go until well after dark. Showers, rest rooms, and a swim area can all be found at the park's northwest corner. This is a great place to

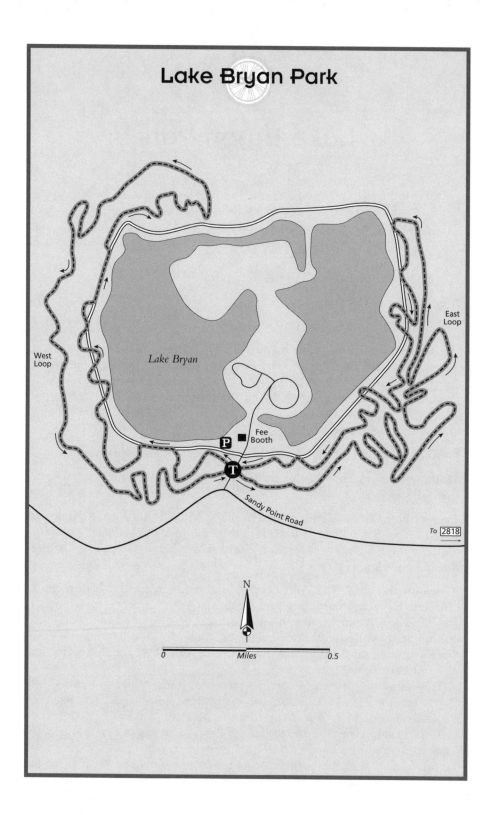

Lake Bryan Park

West
Loop

Lake Bryan

East
Loop

P   ■ Fee
         Booth

T

Sandy Point Road

To 2818

N

0   Miles   0.5

hang out and ride for a couple days. They have also been hosting a NORBA race every year, in case you're getting that competitive itch. One thing's for certain: Do not ride this place if it's wet. The trails are mostly in low-lands that seem as though they'd turn to swamp with any real rain.

The Ride

West Loop

0.0 From the entry station, take the trail heading west. It starts out as sandy singletrack, following the service road that circles the lake. The road, which is more doubletrack than road, sits on a high berm; the trail climbs to it and drops away from it, over and over again. Each split is clearly marked, so you won't miss any sections (unless you want to).

1.0 The trail crosses the road, dropping down and winding around between the road and the lake. It's still a little sandy, but it's fairly fast and quite beautiful down by the water.

1.5 Back at the other side of the road, the trail ducks into the woods. This is the type of tight and winding singletrack that you'll be on all day.

1.7 A quick, steep climb puts you back on the doubletrack. Turn left and follow it for about 0.25 mile. The reentry is well marked.

2.0 Break left at the CAUTION sign, dropping down steeply to the trail in the lowland area. Before you know it, you're climbing to the road again. There's a pattern here, and knowing when you're heading back toward the road really helps prepare you for the climbs, which are all very short but somewhat steep.

2.3 This drop from the doubletrack is a steep one, equipped with hay bale bumpers and everything.

2.7 The trail stays off the road for a bit, passing through a wooded camp area and crossing a dirt road and winding around this thin strip of real estate, touching the lake and darting back away, hitting some small, quick hills and whoop-de-dos.

3.4 The CAUTION sign here signals a heck of a drop into the creekbed and then back across the other side. The surface is really smooth and hard packed, so it looks tougher than it is, but heed the sign nonetheless.

4.1 Follow the arrow to the right, which takes you into some corkscrew singletrack before turning you around for the return trip. There's lots of speedy singletrack to go, though.

5.0 A quick climb leads to a quick drop leads to a long climb—then you fly down a long chute of a trail, smooth surface with a little ramplike hump in it. This'll take you back to your BMX past. You don't hit the doubletrack much on the way back.

6.0   The trail runs between the park road and the dirt road here, with the lake far to the left. The corners in the fast section are nicely banked, so you can keep the cadence up pretty high through them.

6.6   Another steep climb sets you up for a blast down a concrete chute, where you might feel a bit like Robbie Kneivel setting up to jump a string of buses.

7.5   Back at the entry gate. You can either take a break down by the lakeside or jump right on the other loop from here.

East Loop

0.0   This time heading east from the entry station, the trail is again sandy singletrack, but you're thrown into some really fun whoop-de-dos right off the bat.

1.0   Enter the Munnerin Loop across a jeep road. This trail, too, is well marked—fast and winding sandy singletrack that's packed hard enough for the sand not to be an issue. There's a split between the expert and beginner trails because of one somewhat hairy downhill. It's a steep one, but it's doable.

1.9   Wooden bridges and bolstered trails make this a veritable mountain bike playground, every foot of trail thoroughly enjoyable.

2.7   Cross a little wooden bridge that's inclined so steeply on both sides that it looks like a gate at first. The bridge gets you up and over a huge downed tree. Very cool.

2.9   Crossing a road you come to two signs: One says TURBO ROAD and the other says CUT OFF. Take Turbo Road. It starts off as doubletrack but quickly goes single, taking long lines through some soft and sandy terrain that's surprisingly fast.

3.5   Cruise through a grove of big oaks and out into a clearing crossed by power lines.

3.7   The GAME TRAIL sign points you to the right and into a section filled with whoop-de-dos across a fairly deep ravine. The ups and downs are a little bigger than on the West Loop.

4.2   Negotiate a homemade log obstacle.

4.5   Crossing the road again you come to The Flats—and it is. Totally flat. It's like riding on a rail, just carried along with little effort.

5.3   A quick dip down to the left brings you to Skinny Dip Loop on the other side of the road. The trail heads off toward the water and then ducks back, as the other trails do.

5.8   The 7 Back Trail, marked with a black diamond, offers some nice steep switchbacklike sections.

6.1   Coming out of that section you hit another split, where the sport and expert riders go left and the beginners go right. There are some steep rises and drops in this section, lots of speedy back and forth in the trees.

7.0   The trails reconnect and charge through more of the same: fast and tightly packed stretches of ashy singletrack that go on and on.

Oddly enough, this section is almost more difficult than when the beginner and expert trails were separated.

8.5 You'll work your way up and down from the doubletrack a few times on the last stretch of this trail, but you don't spend near as much time on it as with the West Loop. Hitting the Rock Garden at the end of the ride brings you back to where you started.

Double Lake Trail

Location: Sam Houston National Forest, near Coldspring.

Distance: 7.5-mile loop.

Time: 1 hour.

Tread: Singletrack.

Aerobic level: Easy to moderate.

Technical difficulty: 2.

Highlights: An extremely fun, fairly easy, mountain bike–only trail that meanders around the outskirts of the recreation area through the green and scenic Sam Houston National Forest. There's not a whole lot of elevation gain to contend with here, just a lot of tree-shaded twisty turns and flatland pedal spinning.

Land status: National Forest.

Maps: Free map at park headquarters; USGS Coldspring.

Access: Take U.S. 59 north from Houston to FM 2025, just past Cleveland. Head north on FM 2025 (west from U.S. 59, through the National Forest) for 17 miles to the park entrance on the right. Follow the signs to the group camping area and park there.

Notes on the trail: Sure, it's pretty flat. But the lack of hell-bent descents (and the climbs that go along with them) does nothing to diminish the level of plain old fun that you and a group of riding buddies can have on this trail. It's fast and smooth, and there are twists and turns galore—the kind that really make you focus on simple handling skills. Digging into and pedaling through corners are two skills that will most definitely benefit from

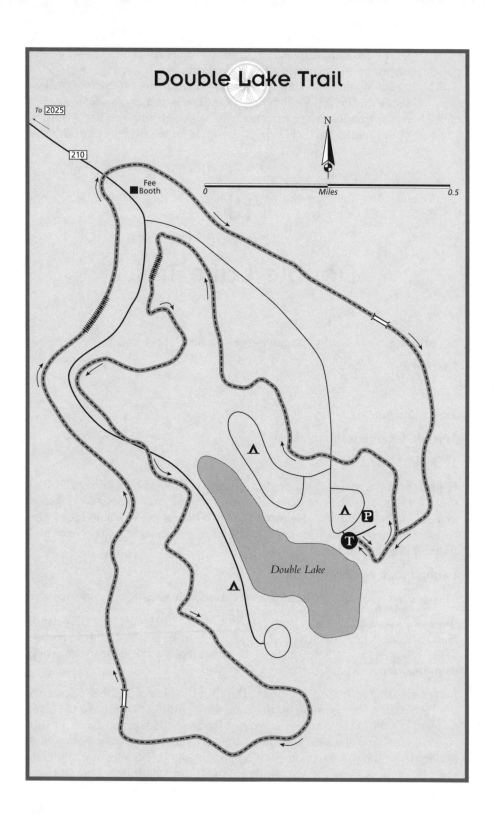

Double Lake Trail

To 2025

210

Fee
Booth

N

0   Miles   0.5

Double Lake

time spent on the Double Lake Trail, not to mention the endurance you'll build from the virtual absence of coasting.

The canopy formed by the pine and maple trees makes for about as serene a setting as you'll find in East Texas, and the terrain, though sandy in a few spots, is consistently smooth and solid, interrupted by some roots and blanketed with leaves. There are also a couple small bridges and a wooden boardwalk along the way.

The mountain bike trailhead is marked only at the trailhead. If you're camping, the park road from the camping area to the trailhead is a great 2-mile warm-up—and you can hop on the trail at any of the crossings.

The Ride

0.0 Trailhead near the group camping area at the end of the road. Look hard for the sign, then head out, away from the lake. The first fork comes quick; take a left here and follow the signs.

0.5 The first road crossing is not marked as a jog to the right, but it *is* a jog to the right. Hit the street and go right; the trail ducks back in to the left after about 30 yards or so.

1.2 Consistent pedaling turns briefly to trudging as the trail gets a little sandy in parts. Here you hit a bed of sand, then a small open field, and then it's back to the hardpack singletrack.

1.3 A little stretch of concrete lattice embedded into the dirt takes you over the creekbed and drainages.

2.1 Cross a long boardwalk of sorts that gets you up off the low, soggy ground. The road is directly to your right again.

2.4 The second road crossing is painted yellow. This one is very near the campsites.

2.7 There are some challenges out here—like this nice log pyramid stacked up in the trail about 3 feet high, with some chain-ring bites taken out of it.

3.2 The trail breaks to the left away from the fire road here. Between the white marks on the trees and the occasional arrows and obvious lay of the trail, it's pretty easy to follow—even head down and zipping back and forth as you will no doubt be.

3.5 Here the trail splits, the bike trail breaking right and a different path going straight to the concession area over by the beach.

4.3 A real, full-size bridge.

4.8 The trail takes a nice dip into a creekbed and back up again. It's no more than a 5-foot drop, but these concrete lattice bits can get a little hairy if they're partially covered with leaves and you can't see the edges.

5.5 Another long boardwalk-type bridge, again right next to the road.

5.9 The trail crosses the road right by the entrance, which is to the right. Right after the crossing it gets really fast, so get those feet turning.

6.8   Another little wooden bridge.

7.4   Back at the fork at the beginning again. It makes for a nice finish—
a long, winding bomb with some bermed corners that allow you
to keep your speed.

7.5   Back at the parking lot.

Huntsville State Park

Location: Huntsville.

Distance: 9.5-mile loop.

Time: 1.5 hours.

Tread: Mostly hardpack singletrack with doubletrack connecting trails.

Aerobic level: Moderate.

Technical difficulty: 3.

Highlights: A fun, fast course for riders of all levels, Huntsville is an East
Texas biker's playground. This place is loaded with lots of smooth singletrack covered with cushy pine needles, and the low swampy areas use
boardwalks to keep you out of the muck.

Land status: State Park.

Maps: Free park map; USGS Huntsville, Moore Grove.

Access: Take I–45 south from Huntsville to exit 109. Go 2 miles to Park
Road 40 and turn right, heading west for about 1.5 miles to the park
entrance.

Notes on the trail: The trail at Huntsville State Park defies one of the
main laws of physics in mountain biking: It seems that the number and
degree of fun of downhill sections on this trail is *not* directly proportional
to the number and degree of leg-burning climbs. In other words, you'll feel
like you're spending more time riding downhill than you are climbing. The
descents are long-and-fast stretches of mostly smooth singletrack that will
have you hooting with unbridled glee, while the ascents are generally
gradual enough to keep you from huffing too hard. Some climbs are criss-
crossed with exposed tree roots, and some of the corners are sandy and

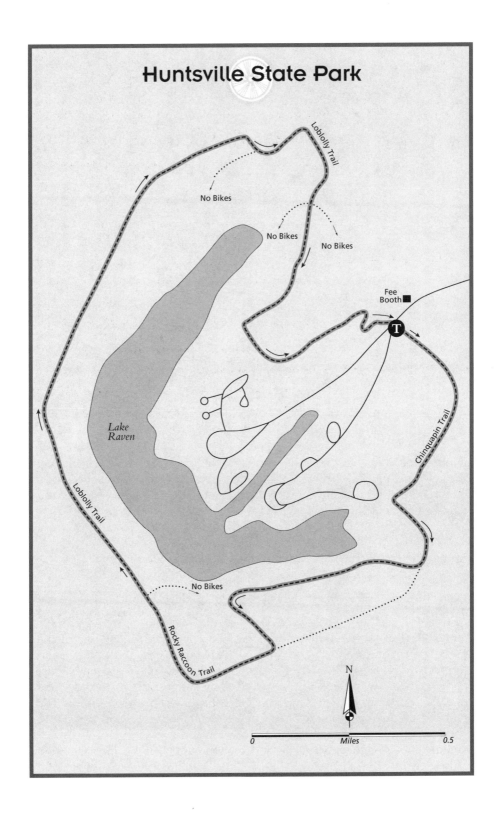

Huntsville State Park

Lobiolly Trail

No Bikes

No Bikes

No Bikes

Fee
Booth

T

Lake
Raven

Lobiolly Trail

Chinquapin Trail

No Bikes

Rocky Raccoon Trail

N

0   Miles   0.5

Brothers Eric and John keeping up the pace at Huntsville State Park. The annual race here is an event not to be missed. Get out there and see what your fellow Texas bikers are up to.

washed out, but the course is technically easy enough for almost anyone to enjoy.

The Ride

Another great thing about this trail is the potential for speed. Long, sweeping hills lead into a wealth of fast, hard-packed singletrack that begs you to keep your feet spinning. It's a quick course, demanding because the lack of obstacles or technical sections urges you to keep moving, faster and faster. Multiple laps are a definite possibility if you're up for a long day in the saddle.

There are many ways to approach this trail. The park map shows which are off-limits to bikes, as do signs on the trail. Huntsville State Park hosts NORBA races, and the course begins across the road from the Interpretive Center trailhead, heading back up the park road and off again to the right down the Chinquapin Trail to connect with the Rocky Raccoon Trail at about 1.2 miles. A right turn starts you around the course in a clockwise direction, hitting segments of the Chinquapin and Dogwood Trails before ending up on the Loblolly Trail, across the road from where you started.

Another 2+-mile section of the Rocky Raccoon Trail, which starts farther northwest on the park road, is out the way you came in.

Whether you're out for an easy ride or want to race, this trail will satisfy you. A lush bed of pine needles covers most of the ground; and the pine, cedar, and oak form a nice canopy that shelters you most of the way. From the elevated pine forests to the boggy lowlands studded with bridges, this is gorgeous East Texas terrain at its most enjoyable. The park has shower facilities and plenty of spots for a nice postride swim in Lake Raven—but watch out for the gators! Camping is a good idea, as the park offers plenty of sites, all near the water.

East Texas Honorable Mention

(I) Lincoln Parish Park

Location: Ruston, Louisiana.

Distance: 10-mile loop.

Time: 1.25 hours.

Tread: Mostly singletrack.

Aerobic level: Moderate to strenuous.

Technical difficulty: 4.

Highlights: Consistently rated one of the best mountain bike trails in the country, the Lincoln Parish Park Trail has everything from rolling piney-woods singletrack to long, leg-busting climbs and intense descents. The beautiful Louisiana setting makes for an extremely pleasant weekend spent on the bike and around the campfire.

Land status: Parish (County) Park.

Maps: Available at the park.

Access: Take I–20 out of Texas and into Louisiana. At Louisiana Highway 22, exit 86, head north about 3 miles to the park entrance on your left. Inside the park, take the park road to the fork and go right, then follow this all the way to the lake. The trail starts out on a jeep trail next to the green sign that says BIKE ROUTE.

Notes on the trail: OK, so this ride isn't in Texas. But it's got an honorary place in the list of the best Texas rides due to its proximity to our state's eastern border—and the fact that the last race of the year in the Texas Cup is usually held here. The trail is awesome, as fun as any other listed in this book. It's definitely worth the trip out.

The ride: The first third of the trail, up to the road crossing, is fairly easy and provides a good warm-up for things to come. Fairly flat and rolling, there are some small hills and a few roots to negotiate but no big problems.

After the first road crossing, the going gets a little tougher. A steep descent leads to a long climb leads to a technical descent leads to a switchback climb . . . you get the picture. There are a few spots where you can put a bit of air between rubber and dirt at high speed, so watch yourself. A climb up Tomac Hill brings you to the last section of the trail, which is much like the first section—traveling through rolling piney woods and gaining and losing only small amounts of elevation at a go.

Appendix A:
Rides at a Glance

Got something specific in mind? The following lists separate the treacherous from the tranquil, the quickie from the tricky, and the gorgeous from the gonzo.

Best Family Rides
12 Pasture Loop
18 Upper Gorman Creek Trail
19 Good Water Trail
22 Walnut Creek
24 Town Lake Hike and Bike
26 Homestead Trail
28 Muleshoe Recreation Area
36 Lake Mineral Wells State Trailway
43 Somerville Trailway
45 Brazos Bend State Park
49 Double Lake Trail

Best Singletrack
9 X Bar Ranch
21 BLORA/Fort Hood Trailblazers Mountain Bike Park
23 Emma Long Motocross Park
25 Barton Creek Greenbelt
29 Rocky Hill Ranch
35 The Breaks at Bar-H Ranch
38 Northshore Trail
40 Cedar Hill State Park Trail
41 Cedar Brake Trail
44 Memorial Park
46 Tyler State Park
48 Lake Bryan Park
50 Huntsville State Park
E Bluff Creek Ranch

Best Climbs
1 Franklin Mountains State Park Trail
16 Flat Rock Ranch
23 Emma Long Motocross Park
46 Tyler State Park

A Lajitas Loop

Best Downhills
2 Oso Loop
16 Flat Rock Ranch
46 Tyler State Park
A Lajitas Loop
C Cameron Park
I Lincoln Parish Park

Best Technical Challenges
13 Hightower Loop
14 Kelly Creek Ranch
21 BLORA/Fort Hood Trailblazers Mountain Bike Park
23 Emma Long Motocross Park
35 The Breaks at Bar-H Ranch
41 Cedar Brake Trail
C Cameron Park

Best Training/Learning Rides
10 Hermit's Trace/Cougar Canyon
22 Walnut Creek
28 Muleshoe Recreation Area
43 Somerville Trailway
47 Martin Creek Lake State Park

Best History Lessons
7 Rio Grande River Trail (Seminole Canyon State Historical Park)
26 Homestead Trail (McKinney Falls State Park)
34 Capitol Peak/Lighthouse Trail (Palo Duro Canyon State Park)
41 Cedar Brake Trail (Dinosaur Valley State Park)

Best Epic Rides

1 Franklin Mountains State Park Trail
2 Oso Loop (Big Bend Ranch State Park)
4 Glenn Spring Loop
16 Flat Rock Ranch
30 Quitaque Canyon/Los Lingos Rails to Trails

Best Short Rides

11 Wilderness Trail/Bandera Creek
15 Kerrville-Schreiner State Park Trail
22 Walnut Creek
26 Homestead Trail

27 Pace Bend Park
39 Knob Hill Trail
H Jack Brooks Park

Best Views

3 Old Maverick Road
5 Old Ore Road
6 Devil's River State Natural Area Trail
7 Rio Grande River Trail
15 Kerrville-Schreiner State Park Trail
17 Wolf Mountain Trail
24 Town Lake Hike and Bike
32 Lower Canyon Trail
B El Solitario Road

Appendix B: Clubs and Organizations

I've heard it said many times: "I don't need to belong to any club to ride a mountain bike." Some people think that belonging to a club or organization goes against the grain of what it means to be a mountain biker—i.e., to be independent, self-sufficient, a free spirit, if you will. Sure. To a certain extent, I can go along with that. But it's also true that without some mountain bike organizations, there would be far fewer places to ride. IMBA (International Mountain Bike Association) is perhaps the best known of these, and the work they've done on the national and international levels has meant that huge populations of riders continue to have access to the trails they love to ride. And love 'em or hate 'em, race circuits would not be what they are without NORBA (National Off Road Bicycle Association). And these are just the big organizations. Local organizations such as the Texas Bicycling Coalition and the Central Texas Trail Tamers work tirelessly to keep trails open and maintained.

So, no, you don't have to belong to a club in order to ride a mountain bike. But there is the larger world of the mountain biking community, of which you are a part, like it or not, and there's more to mountain biking than just putting tire to trail a few times a week. Check it out. These are people with common interests, and they just might turn out to be future friends and riding buddies. We all need those.

The World Wide Web is the best place to look for information about organizations or clubs in your area. Here's the skinny on a few of them.

IMBA

(International Mountain Bike Association)
1121 Broadway, Suite 203
P.O. Box 7578
Boulder, CO 80306
(888) 442-4622
www.imba.com

NORBA

(National Off Road Bicycle Association)
One Olympic Plaza
Colorado Springs, CO 80909
(710) 578-4581
www.usacycling.org

Rails to Trails Conservancy
1400 Sixteenth Street, NW
Suite 300, Department 292
Washington, DC 20036
(202) 797-5400

TMBRA
(Texas Mountain Bike Racing Association)
www.tmbra.org

Texas Bicycle Coalition
P.O. Box 1121
Austin, TX 78767
www.biketexas.org

Central Texas Trail Tamers
P.O. Box 151354
Austin, TX 78715
www.trailtamers.org

DORBA
(Dallas Off Road Bicycle Association)
www.DORBA.org

STORM
(South Texas Off Road Mountain Bikers)
P.O. Box 12371
San Antonio, TX 78212
www.storm-web.org

GHORBA
(Greater Houston Off Road Bicycling Association)
www.ghorba.org

Austin Ridge Riders
www.austinridgeriders.com

BVMBA
(Brazos Valley Mountain Bike Association)
www.bvmba.txcyber.com

Appendix C: State Parks

I said it at the beginning of this book, I've reiterated it many times throughout this book, and here I say it again: The Texas State Parks and Wildlife Department is responsible for some of the best biking trails in this state. Without the state parks system, we would be up the trail without a pedal. Immobile, or worse—roadies! We not only owe the folks responsible for keeping these trails maintained and open to bikes our thanks, we owe them courtesy as we enter any park, responsible behavior during our stay in any park, and careful treatment of any trail we ride. Don't shred wet trails. Don't litter on the trails—and this includes those awful and ubiquitous energy bar and energy gel wrappers. Put your crap back in your pocket, and throw it away where it's *supposed* to be thrown away. Better yet, if you see other people's crap on the trail, pick it up and carry it out with all the righteous indignation you deserve for making the trail a better place.

There are many ways you can help state parks. First and foremost, visit them. There are well over a hundred facilities in the state, and every one of them is worthy of a visit. You can't ride in all of them, but you have to get off the bike sometime, right? If you plan to visit them often, buy a state parks Passport. For $50 you get free entry into all state parks for a year. I never go without one.

One thing to be aware of is that some state parks allow hunting during the winter. When you consider how little public land there is, and how little of that is open to the gigantic hunting population of this state, it's really not so unreasonable. So between November and February or thereabouts, you'll want to call ahead when you plan a visit to a state park.

TPWD has a fantastic Web site with any information you need on any state park you plan to visit. Check it out at www.tpwd.state.tx.us.

Texas Parks and Wildlife Department
4200 Smith School Road
Austin, TX 78744
(800) 792–1112

TPWD Reservation Center
P.O. Box 17488
Austin, TX 78760
(512) 389–8900

About the Author

Christopher Hess moved to Texas after receiving an English degree from Eastern Illinois University. Growing up on the rolling prairies of Illinois taught him that you don't *need* a mountain to mountain bike, and time spent riding all over the Lone Star State—as well as a grueling twelve hours in the saddle in the Leadville Trail 100 Mountain Bike Race—has encouraged that belief. He has lived in South Austin for ten years.

Mild-mannered copyeditor of educational materials by day and *Austin Chronicle* music writer by night, Christopher has managed for years to work just enough to fund his lust for travel. He and his new wife, Cathy, enjoy hanging out at home with their big black hounds, Gus and Henry.

This is Christopher's first book.